A LIFE THAT WINS

A Unique Journey Toward Life Change

MIKE HOLT

Mike Holt

ISBN: 0991547004

ISBN-13: 978-0-9915470-0-5

Printed in the United States of America.

ACKNOWLEDGMENTS

To Christ, the giver of every good gift.

To my wife, Carla. You have walked with me as I've tried to embrace the principles of this book. Your grace has meant everything to me along the way. Love you, babe!

To my children: Jake, Josh, and Hannah Grace. Your lives inspire me to become a better dad and to live what I preach and write. But there's one question: what's my *favorite* thing to do?

To Lee Deloache and David Deloache. Thank you for empowering me to "shoot the ball." To him who is able to do exceedingly, abundantly above all we can ask or imagine! Ephesians 3:20

To my staff and the students of Mission of God Ministries. You guys rock! Thanks for allowing me to disappear for a year to develop this vital aspect of our ministry.

And finally, to Mark Northcutt. Reach the City and *A Life That Wins* wouldn't have become a reality without you. You've pastored me through the seasons of my life, from where most of the insight in this book originated. Thank you for teaching me to persevere in prayer. The best is yet to come!

TABLE OF CONTENTS

INTRODUCTION TO THE CHALLENGE CALLED "CHANGE"

It was five years ago, and I was in a prayer time, dreaming about the launch of our school of missions and evangelism, which we call Missio Dei (http://www.mymissionsjourney.com). I was excited about the thought of sending young adults on missions tours across the United States and even around the world. This was a long-awaited dream I finally felt a release to launch, and I was thrilled, to say the least. In one of my prayer times, I zealously shouted out to God, "God, teach me to work at the next level!" After all, this new adventure would demand a whole new level of leadership I was excited to embrace.

However, I feel like God impressed on my heart, "Mike, I will teach you to work at another level after I have taught you to rest at a new level." At first I was surprised, but I knew exactly what Jesus, the wonderful counselor, was speaking into my life.

The truth is, I have always struggled with creating boundaries in my life to prevent me from personal burnout. In fact, I would say that to this day fatigue is my biggest enemy. Jesus said in John 10:10, "I have come that you may have life and have it more abundantly." However, fatigue and lack of margin are like pouring gasoline on a fire that leaves me burned out, not abundant. My marriage, parenting, and calling suffer terribly. I specifically remember one winter day when I battled with what felt like a deep, dark pit of depression. I finally came to what I have always called "a hinge decision": "I will create margin in my life and allow myself to rest!"

It Takes Only a Small Hinge to Open a Huge Door

Think about the above statement for a moment. Vaults in banks open because of hinges. Pristine palace doors open due to hinges. Even heaven has the pearly gates, and guess what?...They open with hinges. Look at the door in the room where you are sitting. The hinge on that door is what allowed you access to the room. In the same way, hinge decisions give you access to the life God has always wanted and planned for you.

Most doors have three hinges, so perhaps there are two or three decisions that need to be made. Over the course of time, I have created margin in my life through three such decisions. First, I have one week each month when I choose not to travel, speak, or be away from my family. I have learned that I need one week to reclaim family time and rest. Second, I take Friday afternoons off to do one enjoyable activity that isn't ministry related. And third, I'm a night owl, but I finally decided that I would be in bed by midnight to ensure a quality night's sleep. These three decisions, like hinges on a door, have helped John 10:10 become a greater reality in my life. They may not sound big to you, but for me, they have made all the difference in the world and started the domino effect in my life.

The Domino Effect

In their book *The One Thing*, Gary Keller and Jay Papasan describe the domino effect better than anyone I've read up to this point. On November 13, 2009, Weijers Domino Productions achieved the world-record domino fall by lining up approximately 4.5 million dominoes. With the push of one tiny domino, it was estimated that ninety-four thousand joules of energy were released. This is the amount of energy needed for an average-sized male to do 545 push-ups. Each single domino represented a small amount of potential energy. However, the more dominoes were lined up, the more potential energy was accumulated, and the greater the chain reaction was released.

I like to think of a hinge decision as the leading domino. But that's not all. In 1983 Lorne Whitehead wrote in the *American Journal of Physics* that he had discovered that domino falls could topple not only many things but also bigger things. He described that a single domino is capable of bringing down another domino that is actually 50 percent larger. Can you see where this analogy is going? In 2001 a physicist from San Francisco's Exploratorium reproduced Whitehead's experiment by creating eight dominoes out of plywood; each was 50 percent larger than the one before it, and each toppled the domino that followed it. The first domino was two inches tall, and the last was three *feet* tall. Imagine what would have happened if this pattern had kept going? The tenth domino would have been over six feet tall, the twenty-third domino would have been taller than the Eiffel Tower, and the thirty-first domino would have been higher than Mount Everest by three thousand feet. The fifty-seventh domino would have bridged the distance between the earth and the moon![1]

The domino effect has been applied many different ways. For us—or should I say "for me"?—hinge decisions are the small things that have the potential to make all the difference in my life. I love what John Mason says in his book *An Enemy Called Average*. "Little differences make all the difference."[2] Little things, like small dominoes lined up one after another, have the potential to push over larger giants I battle and have a profound ripple effect throughout every area of my life.

I have also experienced what takes place when I'm not doing the small things faithfully. On the one hand, I find myself with John 10:10 unlocked in my life and with wide-open doors in front of me. On the other hand, slammed doors in front of my face appear to lock me out of the fullness I can have in Christ. And the difference could be a domino or two, one or two hinge decisions that make all the difference in the world.

About This book

A Life That Wins provides a unique journey through the lives of six biblical characters, each of whom exemplify a principle of a winning life. We must embrace these principles to fulfill any hinge decision and to ultimately experience the abundant life described in John 10:10. Each day's reading provides a combination of unique insight, practical application, and personal reflection—all of which are vital ingredients for life change. Believers can further empower the process of change by choosing to journey through the book with at least one other believer or small group.

So turn to day one, and let's define a winning life, explore the six areas all hinge decisions fall under, and outline the six biblical principles that undergird a life that wins.

CHAPTER 1:

WEEK 1—MY DECISIVENESS

Day 1: "One Day" Must Become Today!

"You're in terrible shape," the doctor said to the patient. "You've got to do something about it. First, tell your wife to cook more nutritious meals. Stop working like a dog. Also, inform your wife that you're going to make a budget and that she has to stick to it. And have her keep the kids off your back so you can relax. Unless there are some changes like that in your life, you'll probably be dead in a month."

"Doc," the patient said, "this would sound more official coming from you. Could you please call my wife and give her those instructions?"

When the fellow got home, his wife rushed to him.

"I talked to your doctor," she wailed. "Poor man! You've got only thirty days to live."[1]

On some level we can all relate to the punch line of that story. Change is hard and can feel overwhelming. This was certainly true for the characters in the story of Jonathan and his young armor-bearer, found in 1 Samuel 14. I've selected this story because it best highlights the first quality of a winning life: decisiveness. And as you study the story closely, you will see that there are powerful insights we can glean from these individuals who moved on a hinge decision.

Imagine the scene with me for just a moment. The kingdom was slipping from King Saul's fingertips. Raiding parties were on the loose, inflicting fear and despair on God's people. In the midst of this conflict, no spears or any kind of weapon could be found for the Israelites to fight with. In Old Testament days a spear was your protection, and a plowshare was your means of provision. The Israelites had neither.

They were in a state of limited protection and provision. Worse, there was no strong leader to make difficult decisions and declare direction for God's people. Six hundred men were frozen in fear under a tree with no apparent way out. They had no food. No weapons. No answer to the question "What's next?" Nothing. They were just frozen in fear with little faith. Fatigue was settling in, and the web of life was tightening. They might have had fewer than thirty days to live.

Our personal situation probably isn't quite as grave as the Israelites' predicament. On some level, however, we can all relate to trying to balance, juggle, and ultimately struggle with different areas of life all at once. If that isn't our experience, we might relate to the frustration of knowing there must be more but being unsure how to get there. We know there is more we can experience in life and in our relationship with God, and we are hungering for this reality. And still others of us are simply striving to see "good" become "great" in key aspects of our lives. We don't necessarily feel like we're losing—we just desire to win at an even greater level in both our personal and professional lives.

Whatever your scenario may be, this book is for you. And as we start with Day 1 on the journey to follow through on our hinge decision, we must define a winning life, determine that "'one day' must become today," and understand successful goal setting.

What Exactly Is a Winning Life?

For Jonathan and his young armor-bearer, winning in life was simply crossing over from a place of just existing to a place of unlimited and fully realized potential. For us as New Testament believers, Jesus defined this winning life in John 10:10. "I have come that they may have life, and have it to the full." I once heard it said that the word *life* in this passage can stand for LIFE: Living In Fullness Every day. I like that! But to be even more specific, living in fullness every day means the following:

- Living with an awareness of God's presence in my daily life
- Living with God's perspective on my life, circumstances, and world
- Living dependently on God's power and not on my own
- Living out God's principles in the details of daily living
- Living out God's purposes for my life with increasing measure

It can be hard to believe that one hinge decision, as explained in the introduction, can open up God's presence, perspective, power, principles, and purposes for my life. However, I believe that by seeing life change in one area of my life, a ripple effect can start and trigger a desire for explosive spiritual and personal growth. Also, I believe there are certain decisions that are so critical that they can bring us into the reality of John 10:10 like never before—because our failure to follow through with those decisions in the past has quenched this life for so long.

As you read through these six weeks of devotional reading, you will see that, rather than giving you a formula for life change, I have provided what I believe are six critical dynamics that must be instilled in our lives for any life change to truly happen. Simply stated, we don't win just because of the things we do. We win because of the kind of believers we become. I'm challenging us to become mature in the following areas over the next forty days:

- Decisiveness
- Drive
- Direction
- Dependence
- The willingness to dream
- Personal discipline

I believe these Ds are the Ds of a dynamic life, one in which we live in fullness every day. This is the kind of life Jonathan envisioned for God's people, and this is the kind of life Jesus died to give us. So let's start the journey together. Let's make at least one life-changing decision, undergird that decision with these qualities, and see what a difference lasting life change will make. And to do so, "one day" must become today.

One Day

The first two words of 1 Samuel 14 became the catalyst for change—"One day." There was a moment when Jonathan became resolved that things were going to be different. I call this the "go moment." It's the moment when things begin to shift. It's the moment when you and I stop procrastinating and finally stop saying, "One day I will get around to it." That mentality just isn't good enough anymore, and you choose to see procrastination as it really is—an enemy to true and lasting life change. Our hinge decisions and our go moments will usually fall under one of six categories.

- My faith (What is one thing you can do to take your spiritual life to the next level?)
- My family (What is one thing you can do to drastically improve the overall quality of your family?)
- My fitness (What is one thing you can do that will serve as a catalyst to improve your overall health?)
- My freedom (What is one habit you need to break, one hurt you need to let go of, or one person you need to forgive? What is one detrimental mind-set you struggle with that must be renewed through the power of the Holy Spirit and the word of God?)
- My finances (What is one thing you can change in your finances that will help you save more, give more, and plan for your future?)
- My future (What is one professional or career goal you can achieve at your current job that will help you be an even greater asset to your employer? Or do you desire a change in your current career path; and if so, is there a small decision you can make now to help prepare you for this change?)

Understanding How to Make and Keep Goals

You and I can come to a go moment all we want and select a category our hinge decision falls under, but if we don't understand the nature of successfully making and keeping goals, then our go moment will become the beginning of a frustrating journey. Even Jonathan declared the direction he and his armor-bearer would take, and he identified the challenging cliffs they would face along the way. He was strategic with his steps, clearly understanding the path they would need to take to cross over from where they were to where they wanted to be. You and I must be strategic with our hinge decision as well. If not, the chances of failure significantly increase. Here are a few principles of successful goal making:

- Good goals are specific. Don't just say, "I want to lose weight." Say instead, "I want to lose thirty pounds."
- Good goals are measurable. It isn't enough to say, "I'm going to lose thirty pounds." You must say, "I'm going to lose two pounds a week for fifteen weeks."
- Good goals have a time frame and a deadline. "I'm going to lose two pounds a week for fifteen weeks from January first through April fifteenth."
- Good goals are accomplished through planned behavior. "I'm going to lose two pounds a week for fifteen weeks from January first through April fifteenth. I'm going to do so by counting my calories each day and by not eating more than eighteen hundred calories in a twenty-four-hour period. I will also walk thirty minutes a day from 6:30 to 7:00 a.m. at least three days a week." Now *that* is planned behavior.
- Good goals are accomplished through benchmark behaviors. Setting a reasonable deadline to lose a certain amount of weight and planning your behavior to do so are one thing. Setting a deadline to improve things like your marriage is a bit tougher. Losing weight is a matter of math and science. You can come very close to an actual date when a decision is fulfilled by successfully fulfilling planned behaviors. However, issues like marriage, parenting, and growing in areas of personal freedom aren't so scientific. But you can set into motion what I call "benchmark behaviors." These are things you are committed to do on your way to fulfilling your overall goal. A benchmark behavior to improve your marriage could be, "In the next three months time, my wife and I will have a date night at least every

two weeks." By hitting this benchmark, you are more likely to achieve your overall goal of improving your marriage. An example, when it comes to improving your relationship with your kids, could be, "I will spend at least thirty minutes of quality time with each of my kids each week for the next six weeks." Marriage and parenting issues can be complex, to say the least, but establishing benchmark behaviors is a great way to establish momentum toward achieving your overall goal.

- Good goals are incentivized. We don't need to wait to celebrate until the final outcome is accomplished. We need to celebrate along the way. Reward yourself. "When I lose ten pounds, I am going to treat myself to a new outfit." "When I lose ten pounds, I am going to purchase a ticket for the upcoming football game."
- Good goals are written down. I know it would be easy to type them out or punch them into a note on your mobile phone; however, another suggestion to take this discipline to the next level would be handwriting your goals on a three-by-five card, laminating the card, and keeping it on your person through the entire year. His point is well made. We all have dozens of notes in our mobile phones we never look at and dozens of e-mails we have sent ourselves that we've not even opened. If your goals are important to you, do something different with them. Handwrite them and carry your laminated card with you in your pocket. Let the card serve as a reminder and a form of accountability throughout the year.

Goal Setting Is One Thing—Goal Living Is Another

Before we conclude today's reading, we must pause here and realize something important for the believer. Living out life change isn't something we can just do in our own strength. In fact, if there was one Bible verse I could ask you to memorize this week, it would be Philippians 1:12–13. "Therefore continue to work out your salvation with fear and trembling. For it is God who works in you to will and to act according to his good purpose." This is one of my favorite verses in the entire Bible, because it gives us a great definition of how biblical life change takes place.

Simply stated, biblical change is you and me working *out* what God is working *in* our lives. Life change involves our hard work and the work of the Holy Spirit in our lives. We have a responsibility, and so does God. This is our hard work matched with his greater work being done in us. True life change is a partnership between us and God. It ultimately boils down to our willingly participating with what he is already doing in our lives. As I like to say, life change for the believer isn't a matter of willpower. It's a matter of the will empowered by the Holy Spirit.

Conclusion

So "one day" must become today. Make up your mind. Go for it! Listen to what the Holy Spirit is telling you about what needs to change in your life. Hebrews 4:7 says, "Today, if you hear His voice, don't harden your hearts as you did in the day of the rebellion." If God is speaking to you, wholeheartedly embrace his wisdom and council for your life. Answer the two critical questions, allow "one day" to become today, and write out your goals in such a way that you can achieve them. Let's get the ball rolling.

How about You?

1. Fill in the blank with a statement defining where you are versus where you want to go: "During the next forty days, I would like to cross over from ________________ to ___________."
2. Select which area of life you currently desire to improve according to the six areas we talked about today. Now write out your hinge decision here according to the standards outlined in today's reading. Remember, goals are specific and measurable. Confined by a time frame and deadline, they consist of planned or benchmark behaviors, include incentives, and are ultimately written down.

Example of Mike Holt's hinge decision:

I will achieve margin in my life by not traveling during the last week of each month, by implementing a consistent bedtime between 11:00 p.m. and 6:00 a.m., and by taking Friday afternoons off to do something I enjoy. I will reward myself once every three months with a fishing trip to my favorite destination. I will do this for three months straight and then evaluate this new habit. I will then make adjustments with the help of the Holy Spirit, my wife, and my accountability partner.

Personal Outreach Challenge

Each day this week, I will pose a challenge to help those who are committed to the full 1–2–3 Challenge connected to the Reach the City campaign (http://www.reachthecity.com). The 1–2–3 Challenge is for those committed to making one hinge decision, engaging in two discussions with an unchurched person, and doing three days of outreach over a forty-day period.

The two discussions you are challenged to have are quite simple. The first is to share Christ with your life, meaning that you show who Christ is in your day-to-day life by spending time with your unchurched friend in a fun and nonthreatening way. This is called a Matthew Party, based on Luke 5:27-32. Matthew was a tax collector, In Jesus's day and time tax collectors had a bad reputation of being cheapskates and liars. However, when Matthew discovered Jesus, he was so overcome with joy that the first thing he did was throw a big party to introduce all his friends to Christ. A Matthew party is simply a fun get together with your unchurched friend to introduce them to Jesus through your life. It is a cookout, a cup of coffee, a fishing trip or any gathering planned with the intention of building your relationship with an unchurched friend in order to show them who Jesus is. The second is to invite your friend to a church service. That's it. Anyone can do that, and the small group series will empower you to fulfill these two discussions as well as train you to take them to the next level if you choose to do so. All that being said, today's challenge is simple.

Decide on the one unchurched person you plan to reach out to during this forty-day period and write his or her name here:________________

As an additional challenge point, would you be willing to share your hinge decision with that person at some point this week and tell him or her about the book you are reading and this crazy challenge you have committed to? Who knows the doors this could open for you.

Day 2: 1 over 601

As we come to Day 2, we must pause and ask ourselves three vital questions I believe must be answered correctly before embarking on any journey of life change. The first is found in Genesis 3:8–9. "Then the man and his wife heard the sound of The Lord God among the trees of the garden. But The Lord God called to the man, '*Where are you?*'" (emphasis added).

God's pointed question set in motion the unfolding of redemption for mankind.

It was a question Adam needed to answer and one God already knew the answer to. But Adam needed to come clean, become real, and reveal himself to God completely. This, in my opinion, is the starting point for life change. We must be honest about where we are to get where we really desire to be.

The second question is then found in John 5. We pick up the scene with a crippled man who had been lying at the same place, waiting for a miracle for thirty-eight years. He was unable to get into the pool of Siloam, which was a perceived place of healing in New Testament times. Either because of the severity of his condition or the lack of help from others, he simply could never reach this pool at the right moment. Jesus never confirmed or denied the validity of the man's reasons for not being healed. Jesus just looked at him and said, "Do you really want to get well?"

I too have had to come to the point where my "want to" surpassed my excuses for not changing. Jonathan had to come to this point, and so do we all.

Jonathan also had to come to the point of deciding who to take with him on his journey. This is our third question and the one we will explore in today's reading. But for now, pause for a moment and answer these first two questions honestly:

- Where are you?
- Do you really want to get well? Are you willing to do whatever is necessary to experience true life change?

After a moment of honesty with ourselves, we must then understand that success is not only about making up our minds to move—it's about whom we allow to move with us on our journey. Having the right people on board will strengthen your momentum and your resolve toward personal change. So the question must be asked: who are you allowing to sit next to you on this journey through life? As you look to fulfill your hinge decision, let's look at three audiences in your life that can hold you accountable during this forty-day journey. They are your spouse, your Thomas, and your small group.

The Role of My Spouse

Your spouse can be a great source of accountability during these forty days. Actually, it would be great if he or she also made a hinge decision so you could hold each other accountable. You will be shocked at how embarking on a journey like this could bring you and your spouse closer together.

I know this might seem obvious, but I've personally noticed in my own marriage that busyness can keep my spiritual life separate from my wife's. She has her time with God, and I have mine each day, but we never talk much about what God is doing in our lives individually. I'm convicted to admit this reality, especially since I'm a minister, but I have a feeling that I'm not the only one.

I also have a strong conviction, as you will notice throughout this book, that our faith must be prioritized within the home again. This forty-day challenge could be a great start for that priority. In fact, even your children can make a hinge decision. You can help them write out their goals using yesterday's reading as a guideline and laminate a goal card for them to carry in their book bags. Then as a family talk about your hinge decisions each night around the dinner table or before bed. Imagine what that step could do for your family and imagine how that would strengthen your own personal resolve to see this journey through.

Your Thomas

Bringing this forty-day journey into your home is only part of the accountability we all need. I'm a firm believer that men need other men to talk to and that women need other women to talk to. There are just some things we guys need to share with other men, and the same is true for females. And I absolutely cannot describe you the profound impact this type of relationship has had on my life throughout the years. So let me introduce you to Thomas, my accountability partner.

Thomas and I actually went to the same college, graduated with the same major, and even shared a class or two together. During our days in college, however, we weren't friends, and we never even spoke to each other. About ten years after graduation, my wife and I moved to her home city. One Saturday afternoon we attended a birthday party, and there was Thomas. He too had moved back to this city. Funny thing is, though we'd never spoken in college, we actually recognized each other and hit it off like old friends. For about two years we saw each other only in passing until one day when we finally decided to have that lunch we said we would have during that first birthday party.

One lunch led to another every couple of months, and finally we became close friends. Eventually, we explored the idea of actually becoming accountability partners and agreed to meet each week at 8:30 a.m. at Starbucks. We asked each other two specific questions about areas we admitted we needed accountability in and encouraged each other from time to time throughout the week via text messages or short e-mails. This weekly meeting lasts for about an hour, and it has become a lifeline for me and, I believe, for Thomas too.

I don't share my story about Thomas to bore you but to make two points. First, sometimes finding the right person to serve as an accountability partner can take time. And second, once you have found an accountability partner, you must agree on some form of a predictable structure of what those meetings will look like. Otherwise you could end up drinking coffee, shooting the breeze, and never really holding each other accountable to much of anything. You have enjoyed each other's company but really haven't sharpened each other's character.

The Scripture says in Proverbs 27:17, "As iron sharpens iron, so one person sharpens another." The goal is to sharpen each other. I've had the privilege of having a few men who have done this for me in certain seasons of my life (Michael, Mark, Brian, Charles, and my good buddy Gene, who was a lifesaver for me in college). However, I have had to pray and ask God to help me identify the right people to approach for accountability because not everyone is best suited to have this place in my life.

For me, I am enjoying this kind of friendship with Thomas, because he is safe (he isn't a part of my denomination, so I have no pressure of wearing the minister's mask in front of him). He's just a trustworthy guy I can open up to and trust. This is important for me because I'm not naturally a transparent person. He will also ask me the tough questions I have asked him to drill me on. And finally, he and I share some form of common ground. We both have a passion for entrepreneurship and leadership development. Put all that together, and he serves as a great accountability partner.

I'm not sure who God might have serve in this capacity for you. However, I *do* know that God desires for us to sharpen each other and not walk alone in life's journey. If we are serious about this and make accountability a matter of prayer, God will provide someone. One arena where you might want to look for a possible accountability partner is in your small group or even in your church body.

Your Small Group

Perhaps you are already in a small group, or maybe you've just signed up for one through the Reach the City campaign. Your church or your small group is a good first place to survey for a possible accountability partner. Maybe as you go through this forty-day challenge, you will hit if off with someone in your small group who can at least serve as an accountability partner for your one-hinge decision. Perhaps you can meet at least once every two weeks and talk through some of the book material that isn't covered in the small group series, share each other's hinge decision, then encourage each other every couple of weeks over coffee or lunch. See how that develops, then perhaps take it to the next level at the end of this campaign. And if you already know somebody who could serve in that role in your life, there's no better time to approach that individual than during this forty-day period.

Conclusion

Jonathan's armor-bearer looked at him and said, "Go ahead, I am with you heart and soul." To me this one statement describes the overriding character of an accountability partner. I want someone I know is with me heart and soul, and I want to be that kind of person for someone else. For Thomas and me, that means everything we share is safe and confidential. We don't even share the content of our meetings with our spouses. That means we remember each other's needs throughout the week and ask each other about them at the start of each meeting. That also means we aren't afraid to ask each other the hard questions, because ultimately we're there to help protect each other. And when I add my friendship with Thomas to a relationship with my spouse and family, who are also committed to growing spiritually, these special people provide a winning combination to help me win in life.

How about You?

1. Have you shared your hinge decision with your spouse and children? Have they also made a hinge decision? How can your family members hold each other accountable during this forty-day period?

2. Do you already know someone who could serve as an accountability partner in your life? Or do you have someone who could at least serve as an accountability partner as you seek to carry out your hinge decision? What qualities are important to you in an accountability partner?

Personal Outreach Challenge

Today's reading spoke to the nature of true friendship. So my challenge to you today is this: make a commitment to be an even better friend to the unchurched person you are committed to reach through this challenge. Two primary ways come to mind. Serve that person and affirm him or her in some intentional way by the end of this week. Sow some love into your friendship. If a winning life consists of growing as a biblical friend and accountability partner to someone else, then certainly these same qualities will help us influence others for Christ.

Day 3: Don't Tell Daddy

Maybe you've heard about the Desert Storm soldier who, while he was overseas, received a Dear John letter from his girlfriend back home in the States. To add insult to injury, she wrote, "Will you please return my favorite photograph of myself—I need it for my engagement picture in the local newspaper."

The poor guy was devastated, but all his fellow soldiers came to the rescue. They went throughout his unit and collected pictures of everyone's girlfriends and wives. They filled up an entire shoe box and sent it back to the ex-girlfriend along with a note. "Please find your picture, and return the rest—for the life of me, I can't remember which one you were!"[1]

Talk about a strategy to move forward for a heartbroken soldier! Moving forward demands that we learn to stop allowing the past to control our present and our future. Our Bible story continues along these lines with the next phrase in 1 Samuel 14:1. "And he didn't tell his father."

I believe that when Jonathan turned around and saw his father and six hundred men sitting under a pomegranate tree, he saw more than just a physical tree. I believe he saw his family tree. He saw his past and where he'd come from, and he saw some weaknesses in his own father he was refusing to make his own.

I admit that I'm inserting my imagination into this story a bit. However, consider Saul's story for a moment. The Bible says that when King Saul was introduced as the king, he was "Saul, hidden amongst the baggage" (1 Sam. 10:22). Again, this was a physical description that could have very well symbolized the baggage he carried throughout his entire life and kingship. Consider the extreme insecurity Saul displayed in his relationship with David throughout the history of their relationship. In addition, Saul blew his inheritance by his own disobedience. Imagine being someone who could have had it all but ended up with nothing (and for some of you, you come from a dad who *does* have it all, and you've been compared to him your entire life). Saul also carried a very jealous spirit. On more than one occasion, he threw his spear at David because "Saul killed his thousands, but David has killed tens of thousands" (1 Sam. 18:7).

And lastly, Saul consulted a witch, which the Bible calls one of the highest acts of rebellion one can participate in. So Jonathan had to rise not only above insecurity but also above jealousy and rebellion. I think it's safe to say that whether Jonathan thought about his family tree when he looked at the six hundred men frozen beneath the physical tree in our story, surely there were weaknesses and family history at play in the overall story.

We all have a family tree, and we all have things that have been passed on to us, both good and bad. We must learn to embrace the good and overcome the bad. Obviously, not all the bad we have inherited has come from Mom and Dad. Other people, past failures, relationships that didn't work out, insecurities we grew up with, and even our own poor choices have all constructed a "tree" we can easily freeze under. Whatever the case might be, we must stop asking our past for permission to move forward into our future.

One Thing

Breaking free from the past, seizing the present, and striving for the future are so important. The apostle Paul called this the one thing he did daily. "But one thing I do, forgetting about the past, I press on toward the goal for which God has called me heavenward in Christ Jesus" (Phil. 3:13–14). The past haunts us like an invisible enemy in our lives and hinders us from embracing our God-given potential. This can happen in many different ways:

- Past failures cause us to walk so safely through life that we never take God-sized risks.
- The past can also cause us to make decisions to protect our emotions. You lost your job at some point, and now you decide

never to go for that promotion because of a fear of failure. For example, a relationship from your past didn't work out, so you decide to "not put yourself out there again" and choose loneliness over love.

- The past can cause us to become bitter toward others and even ourselves. We forget that the second part of God's great command is to love our neighbor as ourselves. Loving ourselves, in a biblical and humble way, is part of healthy self-esteem. But the past can cause us to live in shame and never forgive ourselves for our mistakes.
- The past can cause you to stray from fully functioning in your gifts and talents. For example, the pastor "hurt you," so now you choose to bury your talents, hide in the pew, and never get fully involved.

The list can go on and on about the past. However, success can also hinder you.

Past successes can cause us to become complacent. Past successes can either build momentum in our lives to go after bigger mountains or cause us to choose the mundane, believing there can never be a bigger giant to slay. Why go for it all when we have enough small successes that make us feel good enough about ourselves to coast through life?

Past successes can cause us to feel superior to others instead of pulling others up to our level of success. We need to realize that empowering others is one of the most fulfilling things we could ever do.

If we're hanging on to the past, our past is still in our present. By living in the past, we will never make up our minds, take another mountain, or move forward into our future. When we let go of the past, we choose not to allow anything to keep us from embracing the potential of our present. We let go of our past and embrace the potential of our present by applying the five Rs of the race set out for us.

The Rs of Our Race

Hebrews 12:1–2 says, "Therefore, since we are surrounded by such a great cloud of witnesses, let us throw off everything that hinders and the sin that so easily entangles. And let us run with perseverance the race marked out for us, fixing our eyes on Jesus, the author and finisher of our faith." Throwing off everything that hinders us, such as issues of our past, requires some intentional effort. This is why we will explore the topic of our past and our past hurts from time to time throughout this book. Healing and freedom are much like the layers of an onion. Sometimes they are peeled off one at a time. This short list of Rs serves as food for thought as we address this issue from time to time throughout the book. They will help us to establish biblical resolve in our lives.

- **Recognize**—You've heard it said, "Knowing is half the battle." What does that mean exactly? It means that realizing *why* you are the way you are and *what* has shaped your thought life gives you a starting point to move forward. It's answering the three questions we explored on Day 1 and Day 2, having that moment when we fully realize what has been, and then determining to move forward.
- **Renew**—There is no transformation without the renewing of the mind, according to Romans 12:2. We must hide the word of God in our hearts, meditate on God and his ways, worship him for his amazing attributes, and choose to think God thoughts throughout our day. We must take captive thoughts that aren't of God and learn to change the channel of our minds to focus on what is pure, lovely, excellent, noble, and praiseworthy (Phil. 4:8).
- **Resist**—The first part of Romans 12:1–2 tells us that we are no longer to conform to the patterns of this world. We are called to the cross of Jesus Christ, not to the culture. We must

put off the old self and clothe ourselves with the Lord Jesus Christ. We must take God's way out during temptation and refuse to think and act according to the patterns of our past. We must resist.

- **Remember and Rally Forward**—Throughout the Bible we are called to remember. (This is the only portion of our past we are allowed to dwell on.) We must remember God's faithfulness to us throughout our lives. The truth is, we would never be here without the grace of God. He has, in one way or another, been with us in our deepest places, shed light into our darkest moments, and lifted us out of our deepest pits. The power of biblical remembrance builds our faith to believe God for a greater future. And then we must rally forward! Get moving. Act on something God has spoken to us and make it a point to intentionally walk out the word of God.
- **Relationship**—Living life with others is vital for every believer's victory. I really hope from yesterday's reading that you have decided to embrace an accountability relationship as part of your spiritual journey. Honesty and transparency before God and others give you a platform to overcome the past. The first part of James 5:16 says we should confess our sin to each other so we might be made whole. This biblical principle is true not only with sin but with any issue. The moment I open up my life and share with others, God is able to come in and set me free. You've heard it said that "God only helps those who help themselves." That's not true. What *is* true is that God only helps those who humble themselves. James 4:10 says, "Humble yourselves before the Lord and he will lift you up." Humility is key. He is close to the brokenhearted and draws near to those who draw near to him in humility. And one way we express humility toward God is by walking in openness before somebody else.

Lids, Lines, and Broken Records

There is one more *R* I didn't mention because it's something that usually grows over time. I admit this is a very elementary example, but imagine the five Rs as the contents of your favorite sandwich: the ham, cheese, lettuce, tomatoes, and onions. What serves as the bread on both sides is this thing called "resolve." Resolve keeps the others in place and our focus on each of the principles above. And no, just because you don't like onions or tomatoes doesn't mean you get to take them off. Freedom takes all five of those Rs with personal resolve holding them all together. So with that in mind, and with the understanding that our resolve usually grows over time, here are three more reasons to become resolved about dealing with your past:

- **Lids**—Our past creates lids in our lives. It's the "glass ceiling" that keeps us living at a lower level. This reminds me of a science experiment once done with gnats. Gnats were placed in a glass jar with a glass top over them for an extended period of time. The gnats would jump for days, trying to get out, but would always hit the glass ceiling. After some time, the glass lid was removed, but because the gnats had been so conditioned to jumping and hitting the glass ceiling, they were unable to jump any higher and escape.[2] What glass ceilings have been so ingrained in your life that they've conditioned you? Are they insecurities? Are they fears? Are they anxiety? If we aren't careful, issues from our past will shape our identity in the present.
- **Lines**—What lines in the sand have you drawn to ensure that you won't get hurt or disappointed again? What decisions, either intentional or unintentional, have you made because of your past? What have you chosen to put off now because of something that happened yesterday?
- **Broken records**—Have you ever surveyed your own thoughts? That could be a scary task because it could reveal patterns that

repeat themselves like a broken record. Maybe you tend to rehearse conversations in your head with those who hurt you deeply. Maybe you constantly call yourself "idiot," "loser," or some other variation of a poor self-image. Or maybe you find yourself constantly thinking that God has forgotten about you in some way or is displeased with you because you've "blown it" too many times. Have you ever considered what you think about? What item from your past is continuously replayed like a broken record in your mind? What thoughts do you have a hard time letting go of ?

Conclusion

I believe Jonathan understood that he had to break away from the family tree, and he was resolved to do so. I believe this task became his "one thing," because he was convinced that he and God's people were made for so much more. I also know that throughout the journey ahead, Jonathan had to resist any temptation to return to the tree, and he had to refuse to succumb to any potential lines, lids, or broken records. Though setting out might have been scary, I'm sure there was a glimmer of hope that sparked in his heart as he started to move. I believe this same spark will happen with you as your feet begin to move and you refuse to freeze under any tree.

How about You?

1. What is one way you know your past is keeping you from your future? Have you resolved that moving forward will be your "one thing"?

2. Which of the five Rs come easily to you (recognize, renew, resist, remember and rally forward, relationship, or resolve)? The hardest? Just how resolved are you? Remember the endpieces of the sandwich.

Personal Outreach Challenge

Today's reading focused on personal resolve as it relates to breaking free from the past and embracing the potential of the present. The same quality is needed when it comes to personal outreach. It's great if you've chosen an unchurched person to reach out to during these forty days, but are you resolved to reach him or her? Do you understand that eternity hangs in the balance over his or her life? Take time today and pray, "God, help me become resolved to reach my one unchurched friend with your help!"

Day 4: Moving on a "Maybe"

At this point in the story, Jonathan refused to freeze under a tree; he made a decision to break away from Daddy's demons and move forward into the future. The only problem was that the future for Jonathan was unknown.

It's one thing to move forward into a sure thing. It's another thing to move forward without knowing where you're going to end up. Most of us who desire to move forward have some idea of what that destination might look like. It can take shape over time, but we generally have enough of an idea to at least get started. But not Jonathan—all he had was a "maybe."

Jonathan and the young armor-bearer set out, carrying with them one fourteen-inch sword that was more like a glorified dagger. Nobody suggested this to them, and no profoundly wise man of God told them they should do this. They had no sign in the sky, not even a confirmation from God. In fact, Jonathan made the statement, "It *may* be the Lord will act on our behalf" (emphasis added). If I had been the young armor-bearer, I might have needed to call a time-out at this point. I would probably have pulled Jonathan to the side and said, "That's all you got? A maybe? A perhaps? Nobody sent you an e-mail confirming this next move? No book you've read can support this type of ridiculous faith? There's no word of encouragement from your pastor? You have *nothing but a maybe*?"

There will always be biblical pillars that will serve as foundations when it comes to discerning God's will. The word of God, the peace of God, and wise counsel from those we trust should always serve as the platform for knowing God's will. However, just because we know we *should* do something doesn't mean we move on it. In fact, we usually don't move very quickly when it comes to issues of faith or personal freedom, as we discussed yesterday. We need confirmation after confirmation and somebody or something to confirm our plans. While all these things are good and should be sought after, there simply comes a time when we must move and do something. There must be a *growing knowing* on the inside of us that "now is the time to move" regardless of whether every *T* is crossed and every *I* is dotted. We must also remember that there is often confirmation in the confrontation, that God is always pleased by our faith, and that ultimately eternal maybes should be a primary motive behind everything we do.

Confirmation in the Confrontation

Sometimes God confirms our steps only when we begin to move. In fact, Jonathan said something quite out of the ordinary in regard to the principle of confirmation. He turned to the armor-bearer and said, "If the Philistines say to us, 'come up to where we are,' that will be our sign God has given them into our hands."

Wait just a second! This is another time-out moment, because that seems backward. If the enemy who can kill you, mock you, and make a fool of you tells you to come real close and look him or her in the eyes, that doesn't seem like much of a confirmation to me. That seems more like a death sentence; however, there is a principle embedded here: sometimes the confirmation is in the confrontation. Sometimes we need to move and get a little closer before we receive our final sign in the sky. Think about the matter in practical terms:

- You want to make a move to go back to school, but you're afraid of not getting accepted or not being able to financially afford it. However, you haven't even made the first call, met with an admissions counselor, or explored financial aid. How can you really make a decision until you get a little closer?
- You want to make a move in the right direction to bring health to your marriage. However, you are so convinced that things will never change that you never take another approach, ask for prayer from your pastor, or even consider meeting with a marriage counselor. You don't even ask your spouse to a no-strings-attached dinner or maybe write an encouraging

letter or send a quick "I love you" text message. Can you really make a decision to give up on your spouse until you look your marriage in the eye and do something different that will bring a different result? You might need to get a little closer and confront your marriage head-on.

- You want to start your own business and have always had the dream to do so. Yet you've never made a move to explore your idea, Google your concept, or even sought to ask someone else in business to give you some input about your idea. Maybe as you move a little closer, whether you should move on this dream at this time of your life may become more obvious.
- You want to make a move into some kind of teaching or leadership position in the church. Yet you're intimidated because you've never done anything like that before. Do you sit, wait, and do nothing? Or do you make a move and speak to your pastor? It might be that the moment you begin to teach is the moment God will connects the dots for you, and a whole new world of purpose and significance opens up in your life. There are times when we need to explore the land, get a little closer, and make a move.

Understand that as you "go for it" and move on a "maybe," your faith always pleases God.

Faith Always Pleases God

Have you ever had one of those cool moments with God when you knew he was teaching you about a particular topic and then did something to put an exclamation point on what he was teaching you? I'll never forget when I finally felt a release to travel full-time as a speaker. I began to take steps, move on certain maybes, and explore the idea that I was indeed hearing the right thing from the Holy Spirit. God continued to confirm each step. Not only that, but in my quiet times, I felt as if God wanted me to study Hebrews 11, the famous hall of faith chapter in the Bible. I studied each story and memorized most of the chapter.

In my transition time to the road, I became eligible for ordination in my denomination. For the ordination service, we were asked to select a minister who had most affected our lives to present us with a new Bible. So there we stood, all the candidates for ordination in a line with our mentors facing us. My mentor in ministry was Mark, who'd been my pastor for ten years and the man I'd worked for as his youth pastor for seven years. Mark is a man of prayer, and as we stood there, I could tell Mark was praying over the moment. He then opened the Bible he was presenting me, put the Bible marker on a certain page, closed it, laid his hand on the Bible, and began to pray for me. It was a truly important moment, but I had no idea where he'd placed the Bible marker. Later that night, as I was walking to my car, I opened the new Bible, and there was the marker, right on Hebrews 11! This event was a tremendous confirmation for my faith and the steps I was taking.

As I glanced down at Hebrews 11, one verse jumped off the page again into my heart. It was one I'd been meditating on for nearly three months. Hebrews 11:6 says, "And without faith it is impossible to please God." The truth is, the confirmation that took place that night in my life was amazing. But the fact that my faith was pleasing God and making him smile pleased me even more. As you move on maybes, take risks, and step out in faith; in both big ways and everyday small ways, know that you are pleasing the Lord.

Eternal Maybes

So far, I've encouraged you only in your personal and temporal maybes. But what about the eternal maybes? Our moving or lack of moving can have eternal consequences in somebody else's life. When it comes to sharing our faith or even being used by God, it is easy for us to shrink back and lose our confidence. Hebrews says, "We are not of those who shrink back and are destroyed, but of those who believe God and are saved!" (Heb. 10:39). Have you ever used shrink-wrap? If so, you know the end result. Shrink-wrap makes things smaller for storage. In the same way, when we shrink back from God-given opportunities to impact somebody else's life, we become smaller and less influential in the kingdom of God. In fact, we can end up in storage. We need to come out of hiding and move on eternal maybes. It may be that a person comes to the Lord or at least one step closer to Christ because of our choices.

Conclusion—Maybe, Maybe Not

There is always fear and sometimes the realistic possibility that our "maybe" (whether personal or eternal) may not work out. The maybe at times will seem like a maybe not. We start out with certainty and end up dealing with uncertainty along the way. Or what's worse, we move, fail, and fall flat on our faces.

I have to ask myself a question: would I rather go for it and fail or never go for it and always wonder about what could have been? Regret is often the feeling we have over some kind of action. It's a feeling of guilt we have over something we did. But there is also regret over inaction and the feeling of guilt over something we *should* have done. Honestly, I don't like feeling guilt in either scenario.

I have to believe that if my heart is to please the Lord, then he is pleased with me even when my maybe doesn't turn out the way I expected. I have to believe he is sovereign enough to handle the unexpected surprises along the way and weave them together for my good. And I have to believe he is good enough to come get me if I have made a wrong turn in pursuing a maybe. I choose to focus my faith on the maybe instead of becoming fearful of a maybe not.

How about You?

1. Is there a maybe you've always wanted to move on and just haven't yet? What has stopped you in the past? What will help you move forward in the present?

2. Have you ever moved on a maybe and ended in disappointment? Has this past experience kept you from moving on another maybe? What will it take for you to gain courage to move now?

Personal Outreach Challenge

For those of you who have committed to having two discussions with an unchurched friend, I'm going to challenge you to do something. As you probably know by now, the two discussions involve sharing Christ by spending time getting to know your unchurched friend. Go eat lunch with him or her. Have coffee. Invite him or her over to the house for dinner.

The second discussion is inviting him or her to a church service. Churches doing the Reach the City campaign are planning a special service during the fifth week of this series, a service especially designed with the unchurched in mind. My challenge to you this week is this: Don't wait! Move now. Invite that one person to church this Sunday.

Why? First, he or she might actually come. Second, he or she may say no, but then you have time to ask him or her again to come on that fifth week called Friends and Family Sunday. In fact, if he or she says no this week, then say, "OK, I will let you off the hook this time. But in a few weeks we are having a Friends and Family Day at my church, and you are coming with me!" Move now. Don't wait to invite your unchurched friend to visit your church.

Day 5: Come Out, Come Out, Wherever You Are

I admit that I have a little bit of an imagination. When I read a story like the one about Jonathan and the young armor-bearer, I always try to put myself in their shoes. What would have gone through my mind if I'd been there? How would I have responded to the challenge before me? What words, either profound or just plain stupid, would have come out of my mouth?

I know I would have been tempted to do one thing, and it's a temptation we've all battled from time to time, and that's to stop halfway. Think about it. At least Jonathan and his armor-bearer were further along than everybody else in the army. I mean, at least they weren't frozen under a tree. Let me put it another way—a more thought-provoking way. Jonathan and his armor-bearer were no longer where they used to have been, but they were certainly not where they *could* have been.

And this is where a lot of believers live their lives, and it's the place I have battled time and time again. Things aren't as bad as they were but certainly not as good as they could be. I live in the world of "OK" instead of the abundant life Christ died for. It's easy to stay "in between" and remain there for a variety of different reasons. One reason may be because I haven't been willing to crawl out of those holes.

The Crawl—"Look, the Hebrews Are Crawling Out of Their Holes"

When the Philistines began to notice Jonathan and the young armor-bearer coming toward them, they offered them a compliment… sort of. "Look, they are crawling out of the holes they have been hiding in." I'm sure they said these words in a jeering and mocking way, but I would take it as a point of affirmation.

I now read that statement, and it causes me to examine my own life. What holes do I hide in? Self-pity? Unbelief ? Hurt? Fear? Sinful habits?

What are the excuses I use that cause me to remain the same instead of becoming who I know I have potential to become? The process of becoming sometimes begins with crawling. Think about crawling in this context:

A baby must crawl before it can walk. However, every healthy baby has a desire to move. In fact, you can even see within babies and toddlers the desire to grow up quickly. It's like every birthday is a badge of honor. Isn't it funny how things tend to reverse over time? When you're young, a birthday is an honor, but when you're old, it becomes a celebration we blush over.

There's no doubt that our perspective and willingness to move can naturally change over time. When you're young, you wake up ready to play and live the day. When you're older, there are times when you wake up and wait for the opportunity to go back to bed. When you're young, you want to try new things and live a life of adventure. As we become older, the mundane can take the place of adventure quite easily. When we're young, we're curious explorers, taking things apart to figure out how they work and then trying to put them back together correctly. When we're older, routine becomes the way of life, and a schedule replaces innovation.

I believe we need to get our childlike faith back on some levels and start desiring a sense of adventure again, even if that means we start all over with crawling again or at least with some baby steps. Remember the phrase made famous from the movie *What about Bob?*—baby steps! And sometimes it's baby *crawl*. But at least you're moving forward. And it's the only way you'll ever get a compliment from the enemy.

Come Out, Come Out, Wherever You Are

When we were little, we played hide-and-seek. One person counted to ten, and the others hid. When the person seeking was done counting, he or she gave two shouts: "Come out, come out, wherever you are!" and "Ready or not, here I come!" I believe God is speaking these words to both Christians and the church as a whole today.

Come out, come out wherever you are! I believe the church is the greatest and most effective organization in the universe, because it isn't really an organization; it's an organism called the body of Christ—an organism that's supposed to live, breathe, and move. Many churches are in hiding and abound with untapped potential. Others feel trapped and need the spirit of Jonathan to come upon them again. There are also believers in hiding with untapped potential, unused gifts, and dormant destinies. We must make a decision to come out of the holes.

Ready or not, here I come! Can you hear Jesus saying these words to the church today? Whether I'm ready, he is coming. And should he come back today, I want him to find me on the move. I want to be fully pursuing God's plan for my life, embracing every promise, and reaching as many people as possible upon his return. I don't want to be found frozen.

I told you that I have an imagination, so bear with me again. Sometimes I wish I could overhear what heaven says about me. The Bible says we are surrounded by "such a great cloud of witnesses." Abraham is one of the witnesses. So are Moses, Noah, and Joshua—and the list goes on and on. I wonder sometimes whether I've ever gotten their attention and given them something to talk about.

Here's another thought. I wonder if I've ever given the enemy something to talk about. Jonathan and his young armor-bearer's faith got their enemy's attention, and I believe my faith can get the attention of my enemy too. My potential doesn't intimidate the devil; everyone has that. However, the enemy takes notice when I start to *move* on my potential. This leaves me pondering a rhetorical question. What have both heaven and hell said about me lately?

Swinging the Sword

The Philistines told Jonathan and the young armor-bearer to come up to where they were. This meant God had confirmed the plan of

Jonathan. I wonder if there was any part of the armor-bearer that maybe hoped this kind of confirmation would never come. After all, that moment carried a lot of weight. I personally have learned this about myself: just because God confirms his plan, that doesn't necessarily guarantee I will keep moving. In fact, permission to keep moving means greater responsibility, energy, and maybe even greater battles and sacrifices. That was the case for the two men in this story.

The Bible says Jonathan and his armor-bearer killed twenty-four men in an area of about half an acre. I recently took a look at a half acre to try to visualize this battle. The first thing I realized was that one-half an acre is a tiny piece of land for this many men fighting at one time. These two men must have done a lot with a little. It must have been a very fast-paced and bloody battle. And it also required the supernatural hand of God helping them. Throughout Scripture, one pattern you will find is a God who calls people to do something in the natural; the moment they begin to obey, he shows up with the supernatural. It was the same here, and it will be the same with you and me. However, I must swing my sword.

Swinging the sword could certainly mean fulfilling my personal responsibility and walking in faithfulness to what God is leading me to. Ephesians 6:10–17 tells us to dress ourselves in the armor of God as we take our stand daily against the schemes of the enemy. It's worth reading since we've just made mention of a very real enemy who takes notice of our steps of faith.

> Finally, be strong in the Lord and in his mighty power. Put on the full armor of God, so that you can take your stand against the devil's schemes. For our struggle is not against flesh and blood, but against the rulers, against the authorities, against the powers of this dark world and against the spiritual forces of evil in the heavenly realms. Therefore put on the full armor of God, so that when the day of evil comes, you may be able to stand your ground, and after you have done everything, to stand.

> Stand firm then, with the belt of truth buckled around your waist, with the breastplate of righteousness in place, and with your feet fitted with the readiness that comes from the gospel of peace. In addition to all this, take up the shield of faith, with which you can extinguish all the flaming arrows of the evil one. Take the helmet of salvation and the *sword of the Spirit, which is the word of God.* (emphasis added)

Notice how the verses end with the sword of the Spirit, which is the word of God. If we are going to fight and be victorious, truly living lives that win, we must know God's word. It is a weapon for battle. When I was in college, I experienced a bout with depression. One of the things I did to overcome it was doing a verse-by-verse study of the book of Philippians. Philippians is known as the book of joy in the New Testament, so I figured that one was a good place to start. Each day for about forty days, in fact, I would read one chapter and meditate on one verse at a time. Literally for forty days I selected forty verses and meditated on them. I followed a simple acronym about this TIME with the Lord.

Truth—I wrote out the verse a few times in my journal.

Intimacy—I made sure to slow myself down and think deeply on this verse. This is called "meditation." With worship music playing in the background as I meditated on this verse, the intimacy I experienced with Christ through those forty days was amazing.

Meaning—I then asked myself, "What does this verse mean for me today and in this season of my life?" Or, "What does this verse mean about the character of God?"

Execute—I then asked myself, "Is there anything I can do to apply this verse to my life today?" Or, "What can I do today to act the opposite of what I'm currently struggling with?" So for me, I made it a point each day to intentionally encourage somebody else. And it's amazing how discouragement faded from my own life.

This plan took me fifteen minutes a day to have a meaningful encounter in his word. Maybe TIME is an acronym you would like to try out too. Philippians, Colossians, and Ephesians are all great books of the Bible to try with this method. Another idea would be to read a chapter from the book of John each day or maybe even a section of each chapter and focus on just one verse within that chapter or section. Grab a journal and follow TIME. Whatever you do, I encourage you to swing your sword during these forty days.

Conclusion

Congrats on finishing the first week of *A Life That Wins*. This week has been all about our decisiveness to fulfill a hinge decision. Let me ask you a question. Is your mind truly made up to move on it? Understand that there are times when God invites us to move, and we must obey. There are other times when we have a desire and invite God to move with us. I believe a decision can happen either way without changing his lordship in our lives. He is looking for a mind that is made up and feet that are willing to take steps of faith. Let's move on a maybe, fulfill a hinge decision, and become decisive in life.

How about You?

Have you ever stopped halfway?

1. Is there a hole you tend to hide in? Have you ever found yourself settling for half way?

2. How are you doing with following through with your hinge decision? Why or why not?

3. Where are you going to read in your Bible during the remaining days of this journey? Do you like the TIME reading method? Is there another method you like better?

Personal Outreach Challenge

Your challenge this week is to take notice of your one unchurched friend and serve him or her in some way. Perhaps you know he or she likes coffee. The next time you're in the drive-through, call your friend on your way to work and buy him or her one too. Or maybe get your friend a five-dollar gift card and say, "I was grabbing a coffee today and thought I'd treat you with a free one tomorrow." I've found that if you're really tuning in to the person you're trying to reach, you'll have more than one idea on how to serve him or her in small ways throughout this forty-day journey.

CHAPTER 2:

WEEK 2—MY DRIVE

Day 1: Driven by Resistance

Our second winning principle of *A Life That Wins* is personal drive. The Amplified Bible paints for us a great portrait of personal drive in Hebrews 12:1. "Therefore then, since we are surrounded by so great a cloud of witnesses (who have borne testimony to the Truth), let us strip off and throw aside every encumbrance (unnecessary weight) and sin which so readily (deftly and cleverly) clings to and entangles us, and let us run with patient endurance and steady and active persistence the appointed course of the race that is set before us." We must run our race with the drive our personal trainer in Hebrews gives us: perseverance, patient endurance, and steady and active persistence.

No one exemplifies a person with personal drive like young David as he approached the towering giant and champion Goliath. The Bible tells us in 1 Samuel 17:48 that as Goliath moved closer to attack, David ran quickly toward the battle to meet him. In fact, throughout the entire story, David is found running, moving quickly, or rising early in the morning to see this giant defeated. Why? What drove David to defeat Goliath?

What drives you to fulfill commitments made to the Lord, such as following through with your hinge decision? What drove David must drive you and me. The first thing, believe it or not, is resistance.

The Path of Most Resistance

It may seem like a contradiction to have "most resistance" as the first motivating factor. After all, who likes resistance? Our culture has negatively influenced Christianity to the point that we've accepted an untruth: the path of least resistance must be God's plan and his path for my life. However, study the Bible, and you often see that the path of most resistance was God's method of teaching dependence on him and growing the faith of his disciples.

On December 29, 1987, a Soviet cosmonaut returned to the earth after 326 days in orbit. He was in good health, which hadn't always been the case in those record-breaking voyages. Five years earlier, touching down after 211 days in space, two cosmonauts suffered from dizziness, high pulse rates, and heart palpitations. They couldn't walk for a week, and after thirty days, they were still undergoing therapy for atrophied muscles and weakened hearts. At zero gravity, the muscles of the body begin to waste away, because there is no resistance. To counteract this problem, the Soviets prescribed a vigorous exercise program for the cosmonauts. They invented the "penguin suit," a running suit laced with elastic bands. The bands resisted every movement the cosmonauts made, forcing them to exert their strength.[1]

We often imagine how good it would be to have a life without difficulty, but God knows better. The easier our lives, the weaker our spiritual and personal fiber; resistance must be in place for strength of any kind to develop.

Personal drive is formed in our lives when we choose to view most resistance and opposition as opportunities. I would go so far as to say that the greater the opposition, the greater the opportunity. At least that's how it played out with David. The odds were against his merely staying alive in the battle with Goliath, much less winning the battle. Consider the following:

- For the army of Israel this was a forty-day challenge that probably felt like four hundred days at times. Ironic, isn't it? You're in the middle of a forty-day challenge yourself. There will be days or possibly weeks that seem to last much longer than you expect.
- Goliath was a champion; verse 4 tells us, he was "a champion named Goliath." Some descriptions focus on the size of Goliath, his being more than nine feet tall, but he was more than a giant. He was a champion killer who had proven success in the bloody and brutal profession of hand-to-hand combat.
- The fight would take place in a valley with Philistines overlooking the battle on one side and Israelites on the other. They weren't fighting, literally and figuratively speaking, on a level playing field.

- Nobody believed David could defeat Goliath. In fact, the story tells us in verse 11 that the Israelites were dismayed and terrified. The atmosphere didn't necessarily lend itself to an audience cheering him on. It was an atmosphere of unbelief David had to contend with.
- And lastly, Goliath was wearing 125 pounds of bronze armor and carried a bronze spear, with the tip of the spear weighing fifteen pounds. David wore a thin tunic and carried a slingshot.

I can imagine David whispering under his breath as he reached into his pouch for a stone. "This giant, covered in bronze, is an opportunity for God to do something golden!"

The Bigger the Goliath, the Bigger the Glory

Opposition grants God greater glory when the battle is won. Giving God glory will become a natural reflex when our giants are finally slain. Just ask the 1980 US Olympic hockey team. The US team, comprising amateurs and collegiate players, was definitely the underdog, but team members defeated the former Soviet Union team, who had won nearly every world championship and Olympic tournament since 1954.

The day before the gold medal game, columnist Dave Anderson wrote in the *New York Times*, "Unless the ice melts, or unless the United States team or another team performs a miracle…the Russians are expected to easily win the Olympic gold medal."[2] A miracle would happen indeed. With ten minutes left, the United States had taken a 4–3 lead and then was able to hold off a Soviet team who fiercely attacked them for the remainder of the game. Finally, the whistle blew, and the crowd went crazy, having witnessed one of the greatest sports upsets of all time. Upon returning to the locker room, the players spontaneously broke into a chorus of "God Bless America," a song that is known for giving God the glory for the blessings we experience in this nation. The act was spontaneous, natural, and unforced. It was simply the right song to sing given the occasion.

There should also be a spontaneous component to our walk with the Lord. Worship should be a natural reflex. Take, for example, the song Moses's sister, Miriam, sang after the Israelites passed through the Red Sea on dry ground and their Egyptian enemies were engulfed by the waters. Miriam sang in Exodus 15:2, "The Lord is my strength and my song; he has become my salvation." Miriam stated what happens when we face resistance with God's help and then overcome. God himself becomes our song. Worship becomes more than a song we sing on Sunday morning, but the Lord himself becomes the song of our lives, and his strength becomes the cornerstone of our very being. As a result of God's faithfulness, we exalt him with our lips, magnify him with our lives, and long to ascribe to the Lord the glory due his name (Ps. 29:2).

The Greater the Goliath, the Greater the Growth

Not only does opposition grant the opportunity for God to receive the greatest measure of glory. Let's face it—we grow the most as believers when we face opposition. First Peter 1:7 states, "These [trials] have come so that your faith, of greater worth than gold, which perishes even though refined by fire, may be proved genuine and may result in praise, glory, and honor when Jesus Christ is revealed" (NIV). We see from this verse that the difficulty of trials will cause personal and spiritual growth that is real and mature, producing a steadfast kind of faith. Interview any strong veteran in the faith, and he or she will tell you this: we grow more in the midst of trials and seasons of difficulty than we do in seasons of ease and comfort.

I pray that you will see how self-centered it is when we live only to escape every trial or difficulty. This type of Christianity will never touch our generation for Christ, because people don't live there. They live in the undesirable reality that comes with a sin-sick world.

Conflict is inevitable in the world we live in. This doesn't contradict biblical Christianity but actually complements and furthers the work of the cross in our lives. Consider the following biblical truths about conflict:

- Conflict will birth compassion in our lives. Second Corinthians 1:3–4 says, "Praise be to the God and Father of our Lord Jesus Christ, the Father of compassion and the God of all comfort who comforts us in all our troubles, so that we can comfort those in any trouble with the comfort we ourselves have received." Don't be surprised if you find yourself experiencing difficulties similar to those of people who are within your reach. The Lord knows that sometimes the only way some people can be reached is if he entrusts a similar difficulty to some of his own. That way our hearts are softened, and we can begin to understand where they live, identify with the pain they are going through, and be willing to walk alongside them.
- Conflict will birth conviction in our lives. Job said it best after all he had been through, with God coming to his rescue. "For I *know* that my redeemer lives, and that in the end he will stand on the earth" (Job 19:25, emphasis added). This knowing, as Job described it, is an internal conviction that is fashioned from external conflict when we remain driven to stand, and after having done everything, to stand! (Eph. 6:13).
- Conflict will birth a calling in our lives. When we are hurt, it is natural to draw back and become overly cautious with people, determined to build sufficient walls that will protect us from future wounds. The Old Testament Joseph could identify with hurt. Yet thirteen years after being betrayed by his brothers, sold into slavery, falsely accused, and thrown into a horrible prison, Joseph declared in Genesis 50:20, "You intended to harm me, but God intended it for good to accomplish what

is now being done, the saving of many lives." During Joseph's journey, God needed to bring very difficult times into his life to open his spiritual eyes, to work into his heart a compassion that would allow him to forgive his family, and to give him a calling that would provide for those who were starving during famine.

The Bigger the Goliath, the Bigger the Grace

Paul's thorn in the flesh, described in 2 Corinthians 12:7–10, has always fascinated me. It is intriguing on many levels, but here is a man whom God allowed to endure something he would describe as tormenting and torturous. We aren't told what his thorn in the flesh was, whether it was some great trouble or physical impairment. The point is, God's grace (his enabling power) is sufficient for us in whatever season of need we find ourselves. In other words the bigger the Goliath we face, the bigger the grace available to face him.

How about You?

1. What Goliath are you personally facing right now in your life?

2. What kind of personal growth can you see developing in you as a result?

3. Drive will form in our lives only if we choose to see opposition as an opportunity. Otherwise we will kick our lives into reverse and run the other way. Have you chosen to see opposition as an opportunity? If so, are you driven and determined to allow conflict to produce compassion, conviction, and calling in your life?

Day 2: Driven by Reverence and Self-Respect

First Samuel 17:10 says, "Then the Philistine said, 'This day I defy the armies of Israel!'" This was the statement Goliath made that started it all, and it's why David was driven to challenge him in a fight to the death. When Golaith defied the armies of Israel he was openly challenging the power and ability of the Israelites to do anything about what he was saying Goliath mocked the courage, ability, and strength of Israel's army and therefore mocked God himself. I believe David's blood began to boil at the brash irreverence with which Goliath issued this challenge. David was driven with a passion for the living God of Israel and determined to reinstall God respect and self-respect back into the hearts of God's people.

Reverence and Fear of the Lord

Many have grossly misunderstood the fear of the Lord. To say we "fear" God doesn't mean we're to be afraid of him and run from his presence. We can define the fear of the Lord as a deep respect for God, a respect that causes us to honor him in the highest way possible in any circumstance or decision we face. It is reverence and wonder for God's greatness and holiness. Proverbs 1:7 gives a contrast between one who has reverence for God and one who is described as a fool. "The fear of the Lord is the beginning of knowledge, but fools despise wisdom and discipline." Jesus said in Matthew 6:33, "Seek first the kingdom of heaven and his righteousness and all these things will be added to you." Fearing God results from seeking him first in every area of my life; this seeking keeps my relationship with him at the center of every decision. And when my deepest desire is to honor him, he provides me with wisdom—a winning strategy in every matter of life.

Perhaps no one has connected better on this idea of fearing the Lord than C. S. Lewis in his Chronicles of Narnia, where he portrayed the Lord Jesus Christ as a lion, as John did in Revelation 5. Lewis described the lion as a figure fierce and powerful yet compassionate. His magnificence was incredible. His wrath was dreadful, yet his love and gentleness were never ending. To be in his presence was awesome. Lewis wrote, "As the Lion passed by they were terribly afraid He would turn and look at them, yet in some strange way they wished He would." Naturally one would be nervous to meet a lion. Someone asked someone who knew this Lion well, "Is He safe?" I find the answer both wise and startling: "Safe? Who said anything about safe? Of course He isn't safe. But He's good. He's the King, I tell you."[1]

Let me give you a word of warning: if we aren't on our guard, we will lose the fear of the Lord in the day and time we are living in. One reason is because of an unbiblical view of the heavenly Father.

Before his conversion Martin Luther, father of the Protestant Reformation, was so petrified by God that he nearly grew to hate him. Luther had a picture of God that was distorted—he could only envision God as the wrathful judge.[2]

Too many people, both churched and unchurched, share the same view of God as Martin Luther. They see him as an angry taskmaster who's just waiting to slap his children on the hand with a ruler the first time they mess up. They mistakenly view God as angry, aloof, and dissatisfied with people.

On the other hand some people try to shape God into only a loving and jovial grandfather, who is so full of love and grace that he never gets angry with sin or even the sinner. He couldn't possibly allow anyone to be condemned to an eternal hell.

Both perceptions of God are unbiblical and gravely dangerous. God isn't waiting to strike us dead, put us in the corner, or whack us over the hand with a ruler. Instead, he is good, and his love endures forever (Ps. 107:1). We are saved by his grace, and this grace teaches us to say no to ungodliness (Titus 2:12). He is a loving heavenly Father who disciplines us, yes, but for our good so we might share in his holiness (Heb. 12:10). At the same time, there is still such a thing as right and wrong, black and white, righteousness and unrighteousness. Sin still grieves the heart of God, and friendship with the world is like committing adultery against him (James 4:4). Jesus is still the only way to heaven, hell is still real, and God the Father remains holy and just.

The book of Proverbs contrasts the wise person with the fool and wastes no time in portraying the difference between those who walk in the fear of the Lord and those who don't. Proverbs 1:29 says of the foolish, "Since they hated knowledge and did not *choose to the fear the Lord*, they would be filled with the fruit of their schemes" (emphasis added). There is a choice to be made when it comes to the fear of the Lord. The choice isn't just a feeling or goose bumps but one we make with how we live. Ephesians 5:15 says, "Be very careful, then how you live—not as unwise but as wise, making the most of every opportunity, because the days are evil." Again, whether we live in the fear of the Lord is a choice.

We Are Created to Have Intimacy with God

Genesis 1:27 says, "So God created man in his image, in the image of God he created him; male and female he created them." Looking in the mirror, we have difficulty grasping the idea that we are created in God's image, but this is true. If I'm indeed his workmanship, created in Christ Jesus to do good works, which he has prepared for me in advance to do, then I'm honored to get busy living and working for him (Ephesians. 2:10). My behavior cannot and shouldn't be separated from my belief in God as my creator. David declared in Psalm 139:14, "I praise you because I am fearfully and wonderfully made; your works are wonderful, I know that fully well." I fear him because I am fearfully and wonderfully made. Truly understanding that God created me and living in this reality cause me to tremble at both his vastness and goodness.

The same God who spun the stars into place knows me by name and has a plan for my life, a plan to prosper me and not to harm me, a plan to give me a hope and a future (Jer. 29:11). If this is the case—and indeed it is—how much more do I want to honor God with my life, driven to be faithful, so when I meet my maker, I will hear him say, "Well done, good and faithful servant" (Matt. 25:21)?

Fearing God as the creator God still sounds so "big" and "out there." However, our fear of God as creator is in fact rooted in our relationship and intimacy with him. This could be the reason why there are two accounts of creation in Genesis 1 and 2. The first account ends in Genesis 2:1—"Thus the heavens and the earth were completed in all their vast array." But then comes Genesis 2:7, which gives us a closer, more intimate look at God's creation of man. "The Lord God formed the man from the dust of the ground and breathed into his nostrils the breath of life, and the man became a living being."

Creation was a face-to-face intimate encounter with God himself. He created us, and his very breath gave us life. Creation was an intimate encounter; if we remove God as the creator from Christianity, this leaves him at a distance from us and puts us at a distance from him. That isn't the type of relationship God ever envisioned for the crown jewel of his creative power. The relationship God has always wanted with each of us is to be close, as it was at creation, and as it would become again through the cross of Calvary.

The cross represented Jesus's all-out commitment to the will of the Father and his all-out commitment to reaching us. It was Jesus who said he came to seek and to save the lost (Luke 19:10). It was Jesus who said he came to provide spiritual wholeness to the perishing (Matt. 9:12). And it was Jesus who said he could do only what he saw the Father doing (John 5:19). Ultimately, what the Father was doing during his time on earth provided us a way back to him through his own Son. Talk about being driven!

Jesus said we must take up the cross and carry within our daily lives the same kind of commitment to him he has toward us (Luke 9:23).

He also said we must lose our lives so we can truly find it (Matt. 10:39). By laying aside an identity rooted in this world, we gain an identity rooted in our relationship with God—rooted and established in love for others and for him (Eph. 3:18). By taking up our cross and following him, Christ becomes our life, and our life is exclusively his. This is the kind of Christianity Jesus died for. This is what drove him while on this earth and kept him on the cross until the price for our sins was paid.

Death Coaching

The life our heavenly Father created and the life Jesus died for us to have is produced in part through our determination to live a consecrated life. What would be a good definition for a consecrated life? To dedicate yourself completely to God's purpose, priorities, processes, power, and person—learning to wholly trust in Jesus Christ for all aspects of life.

When I first started to provide life coaching for individuals and corporate coaching for businesses, I had a startling revelation that would help me shape not only the lives of my clients but also my personal life. It dawned on me that for the believer life coaching was as much about death coaching as anything else. It is teaching the believer to die to himself or herself by refusing to walk in the way of the old man (the former self) and to live a God-fearing life as a new creature in Christ. Colossians 3:5 says, "Put to death, therefore, whatever belongs to your earthly nature." Romans 8:13 says, "But if by the Spirit you put to death the misdeeds of the body, you will live." Ephesians 4:22–24 says it is our responsibility to put off the old self and put on the new self. Finally, Paul said in 1 Corinthians 15:31 that he died daily, making the choice every day to put off selfishness and to live a Christ-centered and God-honoring life.

Dwight L. Moody was a poorly educated, unordained shoe salesman who felt God's call to preach the gospel. Early one morning he and some friends gathered in a hay field for prayer. His friend Henry Varley said these words: "The world has yet to see what God can do with and for and through and in a man who is fully and wholly consecrated to Him."

Moody later recalled the words his friend spoke and realized Varley meant *any* man, not someone educated or brilliant or anything else. Just a man. Moody became one of the great evangelists of modern times. He founded a Bible college and planted Moody Church in Chicago, where believers still meet.[3]

This is what consecration is all about. It's a daily decision to set ourselves apart for God so we can experience his presence more deeply and live out his purposes more powerfully in our lives. Fearing God and being consecrated go hand in hand, and when they do so, there is a sense of peace that defines our upright lives.

Conclusion

This has been a deep day of reading that all began with Goliath defying the Lord and God's people, so you can blame him. With a passion David was driven to see a sense of reverence being upheld in the hearts of God's people. When the fear of the Lord guides us in our hinge decision, we have a deeper motivation to press forward and follow through.

To lose weight to look and feel better is one thing. But to realize we are the temple of the Holy Spirit and are required to take care of God's house is another. To get out of debt is a great goal, but to do so to tithe as God commands and to give more of our resources to missions and faith-based charities is another.

The fear of the Lord will help us in our follow-through, but it will actually center us in our perception of God. We will know that he is both loving and just, and we will aim to live in the reality of both. Biblical fear will actually produce a biblical faith as we are living in light of his full character. I will strive to honor him, understanding that God formed me in my mother's womb, knows me by name, and has counted the hairs on my head. I'm not a number on the planet, my life isn't left to chance, and my faith will be based on relational intimacy, not on religious exercise.

And finally, the Bible teaches us in Proverbs 14:26 that when the fear of the Lord is present in our lives, it builds a strong place where we can be protected against the attack of our fears. "He who fears the Lord has a secure fortress, and for his children it will be a refuge." I cannot embrace him as my creator, look to him as the one who died on the cross for my sins, and commit to a consecrated life without trust. Trust and the fear of the Lord are two sides of the same coin. The safety of trust is a deep knowing that God has me in the palm of his hand, is intimately concerned with the details of my life, and will never be found guilty of abuse or neglect with the trust I place in his care (Rom. 8:28). The fear of the Lord sets me free from earthly fears when I'm living out a biblical faith.

How about You?

1. Do you feel like you have a balanced perception between a God who is loving and a God who is holy?

2. How can the fear of the Lord help you in your follow-through of a hinge decision?

3. How does the fear of the Lord affect your personal drive when it comes to reaching the unchurched?

Day 3: Driven by Reward

In 1 Samuel 17:25–27, we find that David asked about what would be done for the man who killed the champion Goliath. The answer was, "The King will give great wealth to the man who kills him. He will also give him his daughter in marriage and will exempt his father's family from taxes in Israel." What a reward! Tax-free wealth and a beautiful wife are pretty hard to beat—that is, as long as you can beat Goliath.

David essentially asked, "What's in it for me?" and the answer helped to fuel his drive. I know this might sound carnal to some, since the thought of receiving rewards from God makes many believers feel guilty, but rewards are biblical. Hebrews 11:6 says, "And without faith it is impossible to please God, because anyone who comes to him must believe that he exists and that he rewards those who earnestly seek him." As a good heavenly Father, he loves to give good gifts to his children, and he takes delight in rewarding us—both in this life and in the life to come. Although we don't seek him for reward, there's nothing wrong with part of our personal drive coming from a desire to have everything God would have for us.

Recently, my kids asked whether we would take them to Sea World on vacation in Orlando, Florida. I'm not driven at all to see two-thousand-pound whales flop in the water, but something about the whale show intrigued me. Here are massive animals perfectly executing choreographed routines—and do you know what motivates them? Dead fish! To cue the whale to its next routine or to reward the whale for a trick well done, the trainer would flop a dead fish into the whale's mouth. From all appearances, the whale seemed perfectly happy with its reward and moved on to another demonstration to receive yet another glorified sardine. Crazy! I couldn't believe that such a small dead fish would drive such a massive beast of the water. The taste must have had something to do with it.

Scripture says in Psalm 34:8, "Taste and see that the Lord is good." David declared that God is so good that his goodness can be tasted in our lives. Again, he is a good Father, who says in Matthew 7:11, "If you, then, though you are evil, know how to give good gifts to your children, how much more will your Father in heaven give good gifts to those who ask him!" His nature is good, and he wants us to sink our teeth into his goodness. He desires that we experience on a daily basis the rewards he has promised us in his word. The following is a list of ten such rewards:

1. His presence

I know that when we think of rewards, our natural minds tend to think of tangible gifts. However, to King David, who wrote the majority of Psalms, and to those who strive to walk closely with God today, a greater awareness of his presence is reward enough. In the Old Testament Abram left everything to follow the Lord and was tested in his faith to the point of almost sacrificing his own son. God said, "Don't be afraid, Abram. I am your shield, your very great reward" (Gen. 15:1). God said that he himself would be Abram's greatest reward; there would be no presence like his presence and no gift that could ever outweigh his glory experienced on a personal level.

2. His peace

Philippians 4:6–7 says, "Don't be anxious about anything, but in every situation, by prayer and petition, with thanksgiving, present your requests to God. And the peace of God, which transcends all understanding, will guard your hearts and your minds in Christ Jesus." God's presence and his peace seem to go hand in hand, but there is a powerful truth we often overlook in this familiar passage of Scripture. The peace promised to us when we refuse to become anxious and instead diligently seek him is the peace of God. What's amazing is the difference the one little word *of* makes. The peace promised to us is the same peace God possesses. It is his peace.

3. His path

There are seasons when we wrestle to know God's will, but there is a promise for those who seek to honor him with each season of life. Proverbs 3:5–6 was the first passage I memorized as a new believer, and to this day it is one I pray, quote, and remind myself of when I find myself at a crossroads. "Trust in the Lord with all your heart and lean not on your own understanding. In all your ways acknowledge Him, and *he will make your paths straight*" (emphasis added). If I'm faithful to acknowledge him, he is faithful to make my paths straight. Psalm 37:23 says, "The Lord makes firm the steps of the one who delights in him." Firm steps are a promise he has made to us when we faithfully seek him.

4. His planting

We all desire success; in fact, success is something we naturally desire, and it can naturally drive us. Certainly, the drive for success can be prideful and self driven rather than God driven. However, the drive for success can be noble, godly, and even promised by him when pure motives and God's plan intersect in our lives. Proverbs 16:3 says, "Commit to the Lord whatever you do, and he will establish your plans." I love Psalm 1:1–3. "Blessed is the one who doesn't walk in the counsel of the wicked or stand in the way of sinners or sit in the seat of mockers. But his delight is in the law of the Lord, and on his law he meditates day and night. He is like a tree, planted by streams of water, which yields its fruit in season and whose leaf does not wither. *Whatever he does prospers*" (emphasis added).

Psalm 90:17 offers a great prayer for the believer. "May the favor of the Lord our God rest upon us; establish the work of our hands for us—yes, establish the work of our hands." It's a prayer he loves to answer. Just ask David!

5. His protection

Psalm 32:7 says, "You are my hiding place; you will protect me from trouble and surround me with songs of deliverance." There are many verses like this one that promise God's protection over our lives. Although we live in a fallen world where no one is exempt from hardship and trouble, I love the promise of this particular psalm. When I make God my hiding place, the place I diligently run to in times of trouble, I am protected from that trouble taking over and dominating my mind, will, and emotions. Instead, he will fill my heart with a song of deliverance—a song that elevates my confidence level in his character, a song I cling to, and a song that outweighs any suffering or circumstance I'm facing. First John 4:4 declares "greater is he who is in me than he who is in the world." We live in a very real world with a very real enemy, but the Lord's presence within me is greater than the pressure, the pain, and the enemy prowling around me. God's presence is a buffer, a shield, and a source of protection for my life.

Lastly, God promises me protection from myself. Proverbs 4:6 says, "Don't forsake wisdom, and she will protect you; love her, and she will watch over you." His wisdom will protect me from making foolish decisions that will cause me much harm. Thank God for his promise of protection.

6. His provision

Philippians 4:19 says, "And my God will supply all your needs according to the riches of his glory." Paul wrote this verse to the Philippians, who diligently sought to honor God by providing practical needs for the apostle. Paul responded with this reward from heaven. God will meet all my needs, and I will know firsthand his provision in my life. Jesus taught his disciples in Matthew 6:27–33 not to worry about the needs of our daily lives. When we first seek his kingdom, which involves seeking his presence, applying his principles, and receiving his promises, God himself will take care of us.

7. His power

Isaiah 40:31 says, "But they that wait upon the Lord shall renew their strength; they shall mount up with wings as eagles; they shall run, and not be weary; and they shall walk, and not be faint." To wait upon the Lord means to persistently expect, look for, and hope in him. Scripture encourages us to look up—not in a self-help, positive-thinking kind of way based only on ourselves, but to look to him who holds our lives in the palm of his hand. Psalm 121:1–2 says, "I lift my eyes to the mountains where does my help come from? My help comes from the Lord, the Maker of heaven and earth." And Psalm 34:5 says, "Those who look to him are radiant, their faces are never covered with shame." The reward is simple. I constantly look to him, and he constantly fills me with his strength and power. Remember, we have established that David ran to the battle line. The strength and power to do so come from looking to the Lord. David said to Goliath, "You come against me with sword and javelin, but I come against you in the name of the Lord." (1 Sam. 17:45). I run to the battle line because I have confidence in his name. I develop this confidence as I learn to look to him.

8. His practical rewards

There are specific, tangible rewards we can experience when we choose to faithfully follow the Lord's will and his word. The scriptural principle that supports this is the law of sowing and reaping. Galatians 6:7 says, "A man reaps what he sows. Whoever sows to please their flesh, from the flesh will reap destruction; whoever sows to please the Spirit, from the Spirit will reap eternal life." Because we usually use this verse in a negative context, we totally forget the positive rewards that also come our way when we aim to please the Spirit with the details of our lives. This is especially true when it comes to your hinge decision. David received practical rewards for following through with his decision, and you and I will do the same. If our hinge decision revolves around health, on a practical level we will lose weight, feel better, sleep better, and boost our self-esteem.

If the area is finances, God promises to pour out blessings on us when we tithe (Mal. 3:10). If our hinge decision is relational in nature, James 3:18 says that "peacemakers who sow in peace reap a harvest of righteousness." If I'm striving to build the relationship I have with my family and sow peace, love, and understanding, I will reap the same. God's principles have practical rewards and implications in all matters of my life.

9. Paradise

To the thief on the cross next to him, Jesus said, "Today you will be with me in paradise." (Luke 23:43). To those of us who honor Jesus as Lord of our lives, we are promised paradise—heaven! Heaven is real, and Jesus himself calls it "paradise." We are just passing through this world, and the hope of heaven reigning in our hearts can drive us to endure anything on earth if we keep our eyes on Jesus and eternity. Our best life is yet to come.

10. His pleasure

David killed Goliath, but the Scripture doesn't immediately portray David as being in an awards ceremony and receiving a gold medal. Though the rewards might have helped drive him, they weren't his primary motive. Seeing honor restored back to the Lord and his people took preeminence over anything else.

The pleasure we experience when we do the right thing and therefore make God smile becomes a driving force that surpasses any other motivation. Scripture says in Ephesians 5:10, "And find out what pleases the Lord." And when I do so, the internal pleasure I experience is reward enough. But still, God, who is good, desires for us to taste and see his goodness. When I please his heart, he loves to open his hand and reward me. And just like any good father on earth, sometimes he blesses me "just because." It is an incredible experience when our motive to see him smile and his motive to bless his children intersect.

How about You?

1. Do you really believe deep down that God wants to bless you—not just others but you? Have there been disappointments and letdowns that might have left a bad taste in your mouth? Will you allow him to wash your mouth out with his love and goodness so that you might taste and see that he is good?

2. Make a list of ten tangible rewards you will likely receive if you follow through on your hinge decision.

3. Can you list any other promises and rewards that follow believers who persistently seek the Lord with their lives?

Day 4: Driven by Remembrance

If there's one thing that will drive you and me to the battle line, it's the power of remembrance. When Saul questioned David about his ability to face Goliath, David pointed to his track record and ultimately to God's track record. First Samuel 17:34–37 says,

> Your servant has been keeping his father's sheep. When a lion or a bear came and carried off a sheep from the flock. I went after it, struck it, and rescued the sheep from its mouth. When it turned on me, I seized it by its hair, struck it, and killed it. Your servant has killed both the lion and the bear; this uncircumcised Philistine will be like one of them, because he has defied the armies of the living God. The Lord who delivered me from the paw of the lion and the paw of the bear will deliver me from the hand of the Philistine.

David declared that the victories he'd had in the past would help him in his present. Not only that, but he acknowledged God as the true source of any success he had experienced up to that point. He could face Goliath because God's track record could be trusted. Remembering God's faithfulness in your yesterday will only strengthen you in your fight today.

But this was only one principle David would apply in his pursuit of Goliath. The following are six principles from our story to remember as you run to the battle line:

Reminder #1: Be faithful with the details, and you will bump into your destiny.

I love the small details of this story we could easily overlook. David was the son of Jesse, and three of his older brothers had followed King

Saul to war. Jesse instructed David to deliver bread, cheese, and supplies to his brothers—and to bring back a report on the battle. That's how David ended up in the right place at the right time. He was being faithful with details and bumped into his destiny. In fact, 1 Samuel 17:20 tells us he arose early in the morning and ran to meet his brothers. From the tending of his father's sheep to the delivery of cheese, David was driven by faithfulness, and this faithfulness determined his future. And the same is true for you and me.

We cannot underestimate putting one foot in front of the other and being faithful with the details of our daily lives. We don't realize the character being instilled in us to overcome conflict and the discipline being instilled within us that will shape our destiny. Luke 16:10 says, "Whoever can be trusted with very little can also be trusted with very much." This is a biblical principle to embrace. Little leads to much, and faithfulness shapes our future. It's a principle we must remember and run with.

Reminder #2: You must not allow the taunt to become a haunt.

David heard many voices that could have easily defeated his quest before it even began. Four voices could have easily defeated David, and those same voices desire to do the same to us.

- First, there was the voice of the atmosphere. That might sound odd to you, but 1 Samuel 17:11 says that dismay and terror filled the air. I'm sure a boy with a slingshot didn't provide any boost of confidence or a roar of cheers. At best, those in the crowd looked on in silence, exchanging glances of disbelief.
- Second, there was the voice of others. Verse 28 tells us that David's oldest brother degraded him, because David was a shepherd. His brother labeled David's intentions for the future as evil.

- Third, there is our own voice of doubt that can sabotage any effort to grow in our walk with God.
- Lastly, there is the voice of the enemy, the devil, who desires to strike fear into our hearts through deception and despair.

The good news is that David's response to the voice of resistance also applies to any source of negativity we could ever endure. Verse 30 says, "He then turned away to someone else and brought up the same matter." We must do the same. Take our thoughts captive and make them obedient to Christ (2 Cor. 10:5). We must ignore the voice of doubt and declare our drive to anyone who will listen and to a God who says, "Go for it!"

Reminder #3: God uses uncommon preparation for uncommon purpose.

Who would have thought that David, the shepherd, would become David, the mighty warrior, by protecting the flock entrusted to him from lions, tigers, and bears? Early in the morning through late at night, David tended sheep and often protected them from dangerous predators. He had neither shotgun nor rifle, and he didn't overlook the sheep grazing on the fields from a safe deer stand. No, with his shepherd's rod and a slingshot he had to learn skillful precision and sniper-like accuracy if he was to stand a chance. Who knew that one day he would stand before Goliath, applying what he'd learned in one season to seize the opportunity in another season?

Just as it was with David, so it is with us. In certain seasons of life, we have no idea what God is up to. We might ask, "What's the point?" and wonder whether where we are now has anything to do with where we really want to go. The lesson from David's life is a principle we can learn. God uses what we might feel to be a course of uncommon preparation for an uncommon purpose. So stand firm. "Don't despise the days of small beginnings" (Zech. 4:10). Trust that the author and perfecter of your faith will complete every good work in you to make you ready for moments and seasons of his greater will (Heb. 12:2; Phil. 1:6).

Reminder #4: Don't allow common sense to make you common.

David seized the moment and declared to King Saul in verse 32, "Let no one lose heart on account of this Philistine; your servant will go and fight him." Saul, unlike David's brothers, didn't criticize or mock David. Instead he tried to reason with him, using common sense. Verse 33 says, "You are not able to go out and fight against this Philistine and fight him, you are only a boy, and he has been a fighting man from his youth." I don't believe the tone in Saul's voice was harsh or belittling. I just believe he was stating the facts, maybe trying to protect David. David was young; he had no experience in war. And Goliath was a champion killer. However, David didn't allow matters of fact to trump matters of faith.

The same must be true with us. The truth is, there are facts that line up against us. There are circumstances we must consider and wisdom we must exercise. There is a vetting process for determining our course of action—a process that includes prayer, fasting, and wise counsel. But at the end of the day, the facts cannot determine my level of faith. My faith must determine how I respond to the facts, and I must trust that "if God be for me, who can be against me!" (Rom. 8:34). We must simply not allow common sense to make us common when we desire God to use us in uncommon ways. I want to see the things that would line themselves against me in the natural bring forth the supernatural hand of God because of my trust in him. That's a matter of faith over a matter of fact.

Reminder #5: Saul's armor doesn't fit.

If David wasn't careful, he could have entered into an identity crisis at a pretty early age. Verses 14 and 15 tell us David was the youngest of eight boys, and while the three oldest followed Saul, David went back and forth between Saul and his father's sheep. The three words *back and forth* jump out of the story when we think about our own lives. Have you ever felt like you were in a season of "back and forth?" Perhaps you've been back and forth with a pivotal decision. Or maybe you've been back and forth between what you currently do versus what you've always wanted to do. The list can go on and on, but we can all feel the press of back and forth.

That's a tough place to be at any age, especially for a young man who was anointed king, then immediately sent into the wilderness to tend sheep. Talk about possible confusion and frustration! Not only that, but when Saul put his armor on David to help dress him for battle, the armor didn't fit, so David took the armor off. I believe it was more than just the fact that the armor was the wrong size. I believe David reached a point where he was comfortable in his own skin and confident in the character and nature of God. That's true freedom.

Think about how many times we've all tried to impress others, to operate our lives or businesses like someone else, or to compare ourselves to someone to the point that we didn't even like or know who we really were. We must become confident in our own skin, not in an arrogant way, but in a way so that we can look in the mirror and say, "I am OK with me being me, not just because I know who I am, but because I know who he is on the inside of me. I will be faithful in my season of back and forth, and when the time is right, I will trust what God has been doing in me and speaking to me." Saul's armor didn't fit, and the bottom line is this: The testimony of God's faithfulness in my life is the confidence I need to pass whatever test I'm facing.

Reminder #6: I must cut off the giant's head to truly get ahead.

I'm not sure if you're grasping my play on words, but David, at a time when God's people were clearly behind in the battle and losing in life, ended up with a head in his hand. I don't know about you, but when I feel like I'm always behind and always playing catch-up, I sometimes never know whether I will get ahead again. But I love what David did. He allowed his faith to forecast his future. When Goliath came against him and told him in verse 44, "Come here and I'll give your flesh to the birds of the air and the beasts of the field," David one-upped him. He responded in verse 45, "This day the Lord will hand you over to me, and I'll strike you down and cut off your head." OK, that's boldness. Notice that David allowed faith to rise over fear and actually forecasted how the battle would end. He looked at the champion killer and told him he would cut off his head—and actually did so. And guess what? Verse 51 tells us that he ran over to Goliath's dead body and cut off his head. He was driven to make sure Goliath wasn't just dead but good and dead.

We must do the same. There are some hinge decisions that demand "good and dead." If I'm trying to get out of debt, I don't just stop using credit cards; I cut them up. If I'm trying to forgive someone for offending me, I don't just pray about it; I meet with him or her and seek reconciliation face-to-face. If I'm trying to get healthy permanently or at least for the forty days, I don't eat certain foods that always cause me to experience a downslide in my lifestyle habits. Jesus said in Matthew 18:8, "If your hand or your foot causes you to stumble, cut if off and throw it away." That sounds extreme, but Jesus said this: don't just strike it dead; cut it off and make sure it never has dominion over your life again. Do whatever it takes to get "a head"!

How about You?

1. What detail of daily life challenges your faithfulness the most?

2. What voice do you have to guard your heart against the most? What is that voice saying?

3. When it comes to your hinge decision, what is one way you can make sure that anything that might hinder you from following through is "good and dead"?

Day 5: Driven by a Rock

David killed Goliath not only with a rock but with a smooth rock. First Samuel 17:40 says, "Then [David] took his staff in his hand, chose five *smooth* stones from the stream, put them in the pouch of his shepherd's bag and, with his sling in his hand, approached the Philistine" (emphasis added). All stones start out sharp and angular when they first break off the larger rock. Then they are worn down and shaped as they hit against other rocks, and the sharp edges get broken down little by little.

The rocks David chose were perfect for slingshots, and David most certainly used them time and time again to protect his sheep from all types of predators. David reasoned that if they worked then, they would work now.

Second Corinthians 10:4 declares, "The weapons of our warfare aren't carnal, but mighty in God for the pulling down of strongholds." The rocks David placed in his pouch as he faced Goliath were proven and true, and so are the weapons of our spiritual warfare. God hasn't left us without the means to live a victorious Christian life. But we must do as David di in 1 Samuel 17:49. "Reaching into his bag and taking out a stone, he slung it and struck the Philistine on the forehead." There are rocks, timeless truths, and principles we can reach for and apply to our lives to experience the life Jesus means for us to live. The following are just five of many.

Rock #1: Time with God

Spending time with God is probably the most fundamental habit every believer should strive to incorporate into the fabric of his or her daily life. However, it seems to be one of the most neglected habits. Clearly, faithfulness in this discipline is a battle we have all faced, and it requires an intentional effort every day. In our world of busyness, our time with God can suffer, yet it is the very foundation of a life that wins. Colossians 3:16 says, "Let the word of Christ dwell in you richly." The word is a lamp unto our feet and a light unto our path (Ps. 119:105). It safeguards our souls and keeps our ways pure (Ps. 119:11). It is living and active, it will never pass away, and it will keep our lives prosperous and full of his presence (Ps. 1; Matt. 24:35; Heb. 4:12). The list goes on and on, but here is a popular devotional format called SOAP that can help bring to fruition the fruit of a life rooted in God's word. Many believers follow this acronym in their time with God.

(S) Scripture: Write out the verses or part of the verses you're reading for the day.

(O) Observation: What jumps out of the page and leaps into your spirit as you meditate on the Scripture? What revelation from this passage strikes you the most?

(A) Application: How can you apply this Scripture to your life?

(P) Prayer: How can you pray this Scripture over the different areas of your life? What are you specifically praying today?[1]

Jesus said in John 6:33, "The words I speak to you are spirit and they are life." When we spend time with the Lord, his word breathes life into our lives, and we receive strength to live an intentional life.

Rock #2—Time with Others

Hebrews 10:25 says, "Don't forsake the assembly of the righteous." In other words go to church. Yet it is through fellowship with other believers that we gain continued strength to serve the Lord. It is the place where we hear truth for daily living and receive encouragement and community from the body of Christ. D. L. Moody said it well: "Church attendance is as vital to a disciple as a transfusion of rich, healthy blood to a sick man."[2]

Have you ever heard "Murphy's Law for Preachers"?

Law #1: If the weather is extremely bad, church attendance will be down.

Law #2: If the weather is extremely good, church attendance will be down.

Law #3: If the bulletins are in short supply, church attendance will exceed all expectations.[3]

Our local church is to be a place of celebration, a place of application, where we learn to live out his truth, a place of anticipation, community, and hope where together we look for the second coming of Christ. Sounds basic, I know, but believers today are battling greatly because they try to live an isolated Christian life. This was never God's intention. We are the body of Christ, and faithfulness to each other nourishes our faithfulness to the Lord.

Not only do we need one another in a corporate sense, but we all need a brother or sister in Christ who serves as an accountability partner. Proverbs 27:17 says, "As iron sharpens iron, so one person sharpens another." Who sharpens you in this journey called faith? To whom do you share your deepest struggles and secrets? Who is the one person in your life you can call on day or night and with whom you can experience complete freedom to be real? Throughout the 1–2–3 Challenge, you have been urged to attend church six weeks in a row, attend a small group once a week, and meet with an accountability partner at least every two weeks. This might seem like a lifestyle change, but the truth is, our lives are truly changed in the context of community with one another. How are you doing with this commitment?

Rock #3—Rest

Here's another rock that will help us slay giants—the rock of rest. Even God took a day off, and so should we. The danger of stress without rest is that we will become weary and weak. First Peter 5:8 says, "Your enemy the devil prowls around like a roaring lion looking for someone to devour." Lions prowl on prey who are isolated from the rest of the pack and who have some form of weakness in their bodies. The devil's first effort against believers is to isolate us (empower a lack of Rock #2) and then attack us when we are the weakest. There is no doubt that weariness leads to weakness and that rest leads to spiritual resolve. Do you regularly take a day off ? Do you have a hobby you enjoy that helps revive your soul? Do you feel guilty when you stop and rest? If so, why? Rest brings out our very best, and weariness brings out our very worse. We must rest!

Rock #4—Serving Others

I recently read something from the Scripture that leaped into my heart. After Jesus had died and the followers of Christ were perplexed about what to do next, two of them were talking about what had just taken place. Then in Luke 24:19 they made a statement about Jesus that struck me: "He was a prophet, powerful in word *and deed* before God and all the people" (emphasis added). I love it. Jesus was powerful in both word and deed. Matthew 10:45 says Jesus came not to be served but to serve, but the acts of service he performed were powerful and had a life-changing effect on people's lives. I want to serve in such a way.

We've all heard of random acts of kindness, but biblically speaking, there's nothing random about these acts. They have the ability to bring hope and healing in ways we may not even imagine. Martin Luther wrote, "What is it to serve God and to do His will? Nothing else than to show mercy to our neighbor. For it is our neighbor who needs our service; God in heaven needs it not."

Not only that, but I believe serving others has a powerful effect not only on the recipient of our service but also on our own lives. Of course, we don't serve to receive, but there's something natural that happens as a result.

Proverbs 11:25 says, "Whoever refreshes others will himself be refreshed." There's nothing like extending a cup of cool water to others and ending up feeling refreshed ourselves. Our service becomes powerful both to the one we are serving and to our own lives. Service is a rock in our hand we must sling.

Rock #5—Sharing Your Faith

Up to this point, the first four rocks were basic and "easy" to understand and start applying to our lives. This fifth one might seem more challenging, but it is one of the rocks we must sling as a weapon of our warfare. Philemon 6 says, "I pray that you may be active in sharing your faith, so that you will have a full understanding of every good thing we have in Christ." Read that verse again slowly…Paul said that as we reveal Christ to others, Christ reveals himself to us in a greater measure. When I open my mouth and share Christ, something ignites inside me and releases me to grow into different dimensions in my walk with Christ. I become unleashed and hungry for more of God, and as a result a different level of passion is unlocked within me.

Jesus said, "You are the light of the world. A city on a hill cannot be hidden. Neither do people light a lamp and put it under a bowls. Instead they put it on its stand, and it gives light to everyone in the house" (Matt. 5:14–15). If I'm not sharing my faith, I'm in hiding. When I start sharing my faith and become intentional about reaching people, a light bulb seems to goes off inside me. Throughout this forty-day campaign, you have been challenged to have two discussions with one unchurched person in your life. I again encourage you to fulfill this challenge and see what God does inside you as you do so.

Conclusion

David was driven to the battle line because he had confidence that the rocks in his bag could kill Goliath. For us the weapons of our spiritual warfare are many, and we need to use them in our faith. When we do so, we will find that the enemy will flee and that those closest to us will fight a better fight as well. Our story of David and Goliath ends on that note in 1 Samuel 17:51–52. "When the Philistines saw that their hero was dead, they turned and ran. Then the men of Israel and Judah surged forward with a shout and pursued the Philistines to the entrance of Gath."

David's running ultimately caused the enemy to run from God's people and caused God's people to run toward the enemy. Our drive will do the same. James 4:7 says, "Resist the enemy and he will flee from you." I resist him by slinging the right rock at the right time, and he has no choice but to flee. Not only that, but my drive will inspire others to surge forward in their faith. This is how Christianity becomes contagious. This is how an intentional life becomes an influential life and a life that wins begins to win others.

How about You?

1. Which of these rocks do you sling the most? The least? Why? How can you grow in these five areas?

2. How are you doing with fulfilling the second part of the 1–2–3 Challenge? Have you identified and begun praying for the one unchurched person you're going to have two discussions with over the next few weeks?

3. Are you remaining driven about this challenge? Are you remaining faithful to attend church and your small group and to meet one-on-one with your accountability partner?

CHAPTER 3:

WEEK 3 – MY DIRECTION

Day 1: This Time! Setting a Biblical Direction

So far we have discussed two destinations of a life that wins: decisiveness and personal drive. This week our third dynamic of a winning life is biblical direction. Think of direction in terms of a popular phrase many believers and churches use when they desire to go to the next level. You've probably uttered that phrase at one point in regard to your spiritual life, business life, or personal life. Good questions to ask are the following: What does "going to the next level" really look like? How do you get there?

I believe we would all agree that the words *next level* imply that the direction is up. They mean setting a new bar or standard for what our lives are to look like, with the desire to never return to the old standard.

The International Association of Athletics Federations (IAAF) recognized the first world record in the men's pole vault in 1912. As of 2009, the IAAF has ratified seventy-one world records in the event. This long list of world records was given a new standard when Sergei Bubka jumped 6.14 meters (20 feet, 1.75 inches) on July 13, 1994. Once he jumped to that new height, it became the standard for every pole-vaulter.[1]

The standard was set to a new level, and the old record was no longer acceptable. That is also an accurate picture of personal breakthrough—setting a new standard for my life where the old life is no longer lived and accepted as normal.

Just as there is a rigorous training routine to set a new standard in sports, however, there is a rigorous and intentional training we must be willing to endure to reach new heights. First Timothy 4:8 says we should train ourselves to be godly. This training takes place in the arena called life and is often met with fierce opposition.

Refusing to Remain "Just as You Are"

As a traveling speaker, I'm blessed with the opportunity to travel to some pretty unique places. One of them is Savannah, Georgia. The culture is fascinating, the food is fantastic, and the city is rich with interesting history.

During revival services, in which I was the guest speaker, I experienced Savannah in a completely different way. To the observer or casual attender of the services, I'm sure all appeared great. But to me, the speaker, I was on a never-ending roller coaster of spiritual highs and lows. One night was absolutely amazing, and it felt like heaven itself. The next night felt totally the opposite. Any momentum we had gained was gone or, even worse, felt as though we'd digressed and gone backward the next night.

As the week progressed, it became apparent that what we were up against was more than people being tired from hectic schedules and hard days at work. I believed the problem was spiritual in nature, and to be honest, it bugged me…It bugged me bad—so much so that I wrestled in prayer until the wee hours of the night after concluding one of the services. I eventually fell asleep, restless, and three hours later woke up feeling even more restless. I then did something I'd never done before. I Googled the city of Savannah to learn a little more about its history and the place I was calling home for the week. What I found fascinated me.

The city has a long-held reputation of spiritism and occult practices. As I was scrolling through some of the history of Savannah, I read an article that contained one line that leaped off the page and confirmed everything I was battling in my spirit.

The article explained that in the early nineteenth century, a departing newspaper publisher, embittered by the poor reception of his weekly paper, cursed the city. "I leave you, Savannah, a curse that is far the worst of all curses—to remain just as you are."[2]

That one phrase—"to remain just as you are"—summed up my experiences and brought definition to the battle we were facing.

What I was experiencing all week could have been easily defined as "one step forward and two steps back." To describe the problem in a different way, it was the deep frustration felt by those who just couldn't experience the breakthrough they so desperately needed for their lives.

I'm not saying this curse by one man from the nineteenth century has had—or ever will have—a hold over the city. I'm not even saying this one statement validates or invalidates any particular theology on spiritual warfare. It's important to me that you know I'm not some hyperspiritual fruitcake who chases demons under every tree and every circumstance of life.

However, I *am* saying that churches and believers can relate to the feeling of "remaining just as we are." On a merely natural and human level, we can all relate to the difficulty of achieving true life change. We can all relate to the frustration of one step forward and two steps back. If not, we can all relate to blind spots when driving our vehicles. You know what a blind spot is, don't you? It's that place in your side mirror where another vehicle is concealed from your line of sight. The blind spot sounds small, but it can have huge implications for us when driving—especially when we fail to look over our shoulder before changing lanes. If we aren't careful to check our blind spot, the blind spot can cause some serious wreckage.

The same is true when it comes to the blind spots of our lives. Things such as hurt not dealt with, unforgiveness, or secret sins could all serve as blind spots. I have learned that these things will remain in hiding until we try to grow and move forward in life. At the opportune time, they can rear their ugly heads and prohibit true change from ever developing in our lives.

This is where the story of Leah becomes so powerful in Genesis 29:15–35. The life of a lady who could easily be overlooked in Scripture reveals the very process we must remain engaged in to achieve lasting life change and overcome any blind spots in life.

Consider her story for a minute. She was the oldest child of Laban, the scheming and manipulative uncle of Jacob. Leah was also the older sister of the very attractive younger sister named Rachel. After deceiving his brother, Esau, out of his birthright and blessing, Esau fled for his life and ended up on his Uncle Laban's farm. He immediately took note of Rachel. Genesis 29:17–18 tells us in plain and simple terms, "Leah had weak eyes, but Rachel was lovely in form, and beautiful." Jacob fell in love with Rachel and offered to work seven years in exchange for her hand in marriage.

At the end of the seven years, he was ready for his reward, but Laban had his own sinister plan. On Rachel and Jacob's wedding day, Laban waited for the right moment when Jacob was extremely vulnerable and switched Rachel with Leah in the bridal chamber. Jacob woke up, and verse 25 says, "When morning came, there was Leah!" After his first night as a married man, Jacob was shocked to discover Leah next to him instead of Rachel. Can you imagine the level of anger, disappointment, rejection, and insult Jacob would have directed at Leah as he tried to figure out what had just happened? Three things were for sure: Laban had deceived him, Jacob was disappointed with his new bride beyond words, and Leah was degraded in the midst of it all.

Can you relate to ever feeling like you're always second? Have you ever experienced just how dangerous the comparison game really is? Women compare themselves to the beauty of other women. Men compare themselves to the success of other men. Couples can easily get caught up in the deadly trap of keeping up with the Joneses. Leah had embraced this kind of pattern her entire life and was now the recipient of one of the worse scenarios any woman could experience.

However, she made a decision to rise above damaging emotional scars. The shadows could have followed her for the rest of her life, but she chose to rise above them. Easily, her life could have been defined as a life of one step forward and two steps backward, but she chose to find a different stride. She could have easily remained just as she was forever, but she became willing to endure a difficult but rewarding process of true change. Leah made the decision (the hinge decision) to rise above the hurt when she declared two powerful words that would change everything: "this time."

This Time

Leah utters her life-changing decision after three failed attempts to win the approval and affection of her husband. The failed attempts were actually through the birthing of three sons.

In Old Testament days, to give birth to a son was the mark of honor for a woman because it was vital to the carrying on of the family legacy. The man would naturally grant the wife an even deeper level of respect and love because the birth of a son was attributed to the blessing of God on them. But not with Leah. In fact, with the birth of each son she unsuccessfully tried to gain respect, love, and approval from Jacob—which, sad to say, wasn't achieved.

Finally, after son number three, enough was enough. In Genesis 29:35, she declared, "*This time* I will praise the Lord" (emphasis added). She made a hinge decision, she formed personal drive from her deep frustration, and she was given a different perspective in life through biblical direction. It was time to move up to the next level. But it took three sons to get to this point. Amazingly, each of the son's names revealed a different stage of freedom she experienced on her way to permanent and lasting change. She basically named these "stages of freedom" for us from her own personal journey. These names were the following:

- Reuben, whose name means "see, a son"
- Simeon, whose name means "one who hears"
- Levi, which means "attached"
- And Judah, which means "praise"[3]

These four names reveal powerful truths about life change. At this point let me bring to your attention that her life change didn't happen overnight. There was a progression of freedom and breakthrough for Leah. If we are honest, the same is true for us 90 percent of the time. There are levels of freedom when it comes to achieving the next level and setting a new standard for our lives. Think about four of them in light of these four names again.

- Reuben, whose name means "see, a son," reveals the power of perception in our lives. The name Reuben sounds like the

Hebrew for "he has seen my misery." She named her son after a character trait of God. He loved her, he saw her, and he gave her a son to show and demonstrate his love. This was a profound breakthrough for Leah, considering that she was living with a husband who preferred her sister. Though Leah's own father and husband overlooked her, she came to realize God would never overlook her. He always saw her and, as Psalm 139:2 says, perceived her thoughts from afar. Not only did she come to terms with God's seeing her, but she also embraced the realization that he saw her with love and approval. This first stage of freedom was all about how we perceive God in the midst of our battle. A biblical perception of God, along with a biblical perception of herself, would be the first step in her life change.

- Simeon, whose name means "one who hears," reveals the power of biblical prayer. I use the term "biblical prayer" for a reason and will explain further on Day 17. There are some misconceptions about the topic of prayer we will address, but the punch line is this: Leah exercised transparent prayer and pressed in to the Lord with her deepest hurts.
- The name Levi means "attached." Remember, Leah was looking for "attachment" to her husband, but it never happened. In fact, she needed to break the unhealthy emotional pattern of trying to earn Jacob's love. The truth is, we all can have patterns that might need to be broken. A "this time" kind of decision is about first breaking these attachments to ungodly patterns and then learning to live out biblical patterns outlined for us in God's word. Jesus said in John 8:32, "If you hold to my teaching, then you are my disciples. You will know the truth and the truth will make you free." By holding to the teachings of God's word and living out biblical commands, we break ungodly patterns and attach ourselves to godly principles, which help us to move forward in life.

- And finally, there is Judah, whose name means "praise." Leah said in Genesis 29:28, "This time I will praise the Lord." In other words, "I am moving on, never to go back and never to return to that old standard of living." There are biblical guidelines to maintaining our freedom once we have begun to experience life at the next level. We will talk about those on Day 19.

Conclusion

I admit that this is an interesting story from which to glean such powerful biblical truth, but it really sums up the definition of a winning life. A winning life could easily be defined as living with an accurate biblical perception of our lives while embracing biblical patterns and executing biblical prayer and praise on a daily basis. By doing so, we will set a new bar, a new standard, and never return to the old one. And when we do, others will strive for the same.

Just as Sergei Bubka set the record for the pole vault and set a new standard for everyone who would follow, new standards in our lives are bound to influence the lives of those around us. Our intentional lives will become influential ones, and our winning lives will win others to Christ. I desperately want this reality in my life. How about you? It's time to come into a "this time" season.

How about You?

1. Have you ever experienced the frustration of going one step forward and two steps back? Can you relate to the feeling of remaining just as you are? If so, in what specific areas of your life have you felt this way?

2. Have you ever experienced a "crash" when you tried to move forward in life? In other words, was there something hiding in your blind spot that prohibited you from really changing gears and growing in your walk with God?

3. Which of the above names or levels of freedom do you think describe you? Do you really need to learn biblical perception, biblical patterns, biblical prayer, or biblical praise in this season of your life?

Day 2: The Power of Perception

Genesis 29 describes Leah as having weak or delicate eyes. Though this is a physical description, it might be a metaphor for an emotional description as well. Having compared herself to a more attractive sister her entire life, Leah probably grew up with insecurities. And as an adult, her new husband didn't desire her.

If we aren't careful, we too will fail to see our lives accurately from a biblical perspective when we try to fulfill our needs solely with the things of this world. Leah became determined to earn her husband's love through childbearing. Although this strategy didn't manufacture a loving marriage, it became a journey of self-discovery, and each child she birthed represented a new level of freedom from her emotional baggage.

She named the first child Reuben, which means "see, a son." As I mentioned yesterday, in the Hebrew language, the name sounds like the Hebrew meaning for "the Lord sees me" or "he has seen my misery." Imagine what that meant for Leah. The one who felt overlooked was now being seen by the God of heaven. She began to realize that she was the object of his affection, and although others in some ways disfavored her, God was *for* her. In fact, he was so for her that he gave her a son, which in Old Testament days was a huge mark of honor for a woman.

What was true for Leah is true for us. How did God prove his love for us in the New Testament? He gave us a son—his Son! If Leah had a shift in her perspective when she gave birth to her own son, how much more should we have a shift in our perspective about the issues of life as a result of God's giving us *his* Son? He has proven that he is for us.

Romans 8:31 says, "If God be for us, who can be against us?" We've probably read this passage a hundred times and even heard pastors preach about it. I've realized that just because I know a Bible passage with my head doesn't mean I believe it deep down in my heart. Do I truly believe, as Paul continues in this passage, that nothing will be able to separate me from the love of God that is in Christ Jesus my Lord? As a friend of mine once told me, "God is not mad *at* me; he is mad *about* me!" This shift of perspective can be the difference between breaking under the weight of life or breaking through as Leah did. His love is our confidence to endure any conflict and our strength to endure any time of challenge.

Oil beneath the Soil

Many of us consent, at least on some level, that God loves us. But our issue is more about the perception we carry about ourselves. This poor perception keeps us from realizing who we really are in Christ.

Poor perception reminds me of a story about a man named Mr. Yates who owned barren property in Texas during the Great Depression. The land was virtually useless, unable to produce any life-giving crops. Not only that, but Mr. Yates was bankrupt and on the verge of suicide.

One day two men knocked on his door, asking if they could run geological tests to determine whether a reservoir of oil lay beneath the surface of his barren ground. Sure enough, it was. In one day's time, Mr. Yates became a wealthy man. When asked how it felt to go from rags to riches and become a millionaire overnight, Mr. Yates responded, "Actually, I was always a millionaire. I just didn't realize it! There was always oil beneath the soil. It just needed to be discovered."[1]

As believers we too must discover there is oil beneath the soil. This oil is our identity in Christ. It is who we are in him and who he is in us. This hidden reservoir of oil must be discovered if we are ever to have any chance of living it out.

We have lived long enough with the labels of "unworthy," "unwanted," and "failure." Such labels only produce a barren spiritual landscape void of the abundant life Jesus died for. The truth is, we are spiritually wealthy; we just haven't perceived ourselves in this light yet. We might need some vision therapy.

Vision Therapy

My seven-year-old daughter has slight astigmatism, which produces a lazy eye when she's tired. In our effort to provide the best care for her, we made an appointment with a doctor to see what could be done to correct the problem. And as we had anticipated, she was prescribed glasses to correct the problem. After a year of wearing the glasses, we made a follow-up appointment to evaluate how much the problem had been corrected. To everyone's disappointment, the ophthalmologist's examination determined there wasn't enough improvement, so she was referred to "vision therapy." I had never heard of vision therapy before, but as we've learned, it is an entire set of exercises that coordinate one's eyes to focus on the same thing at the same time until the picture becomes clear.

Likewise, in our spiritual lives there are a few exercises or spiritual disciplines we can use to help correct our false perceptions.

The first exercise is meditation. Psalm 1:1–2 says, "Blessed is the man who does not walk in the counsel of the wicked or stand in the way of sinners or sit in the seat of mockers. But his delight is in the law of the Lord, and on his law he meditates day and night. He is like a tree planted by streams of water, which yields its fruit in season and whose leaf does not wither. Whatever he does prospers." A good definition of the word *meditate* is to think deeply on a verse and allow his word to penetrate our hearts, producing a deeper understanding of truth that can transform our lives. Meditation is the catalyst by which truth is transferred from our heads to our hearts, and head knowledge then becomes deep heart knowledge. In other words, information we've always agreed to in our heads becomes revelation we believe in our hearts.

The second exercise is eye-opening revelation. Paul understood the need for believers to experience eye-opening revelation when he prayed for the Ephesians in 1:17–18. "I keep asking that the God of our Lord Jesus Christ, the glorious Father, may give you the Spirit of wisdom and revelation, so that you may know him better. I pray also that the eyes of your heart may be enlightened that you may know the hope to which he has called you, the riches of his glorious inheritance in the saints, and his incomparably great power for us who believe." Paul said that the hope, power, and inheritance that are ours in Christ Jesus are so vast that we actually need the help of the Holy Spirit to increasingly reveal them to us. This is something we can pray for, and God loves to provide for us.

He wants us to have those "aha!" kinds of moments, when our eyes are opened to see him and we understand ourselves as portrayed in his word. Meditation and revelation guard our perception of God and ourselves.

However, seeking accurate information in turn guards our relationships and our perceptions of others—which is our third exercise for vision therapy. This doesn't sound nearly as spiritual as revelation, but it's very powerful when it comes to dealing with conflict in relationships. Psalm 5:8 tells us to seek peace and pursue it. Matthew 18 outlines the proper way to deal with issues in our relationships, and the book of Proverbs is full of practical wisdom to guide us in our affairs with others. James 1:19 says to be quick to listen, slow to speak, and slow to become angry. We fulfill these verses by listening and seeking to understand others.

This could mean something as simple as "clearing the air" or asking someone to explain what he or she meant before we jump to conclusions. In all cases our motive must be aimed toward peace and understanding. As my pastor used to tell me, misunderstanding is the death knell of all relationships. Understanding, then, is the ultimate safeguard.

What's important to note is that we must process all information through the filter of God's grace. I've come to understand that once I have a revelation of God's love and grace for me, extending grace to others is easier for me. Failure to do so, according to Jesus, is a high form of hypocrisy. He requires me to extend the same grace to others that I have received from him—which ensures the ability to keep my relationships from falling apart.

The last spiritual discipline that will produce a biblical perspective is simply an application of God's word in the details of my daily life. James 1:22–25 says, "Don't merely listen to the Word, and so deceive ourselves. Do what it says. Anyone who listens to the Word but doesn't do what it says is like someone who looks at his face in a mirror and, after looking at himself, goes away and immediately forgets what he looks like." Disobedience can cause great disillusionment in our lives because of our natural leaning to justify and rationalize our behavior. This leaning confuses our convictions not only about right and wrong but also ultimately about his purpose and what's best for our lives.

James continues to say in verse 25, "But whoever looks intently into the perfect law that gives freedom, and continues in it—not forgetting what they have heard, but doing it—they will be blessed in what they do." Continuing to do God's word brings us into an even greater experience of blessing and wholeness, because then we will have first-hand knowledge of his word at work in our lives. As you intentionally continue to do God's word, you will experience peace that comes with obedience, worship with a scriptural worldview, and convictions about morality and life's meaning (serving him) that will be biblically accurate.

Meditation, revelation, information, and application are all part of forming and maintaining a solid, biblical perspective. Leah had her first of many breakthroughs when she recognized God as a God who saw her. His eye was on her, and her recognition of that fact was the first revelation in a process of healing that would conclude with "This time, I will praise the Lord!" Revelation led to application. Leah would experience a freedom she had longed for her entire life. The same can be true for you.

Food for Thought

When a person wants to lose weight, a dietitian might suggest keeping a food journal. It can be a very eye-opening experience to see just how many calories one consumes each day. Many people have been relieved of allergies and other illnesses just by closely monitoring the foods they have subtracted or added to their diets. And when someone really wants to gain muscle, a personal trainer will have him or her closely record the exercises, weight, and the number of reps he or she does to build each muscle group. If a food journal and workout journal can do wonders, how much more a focus journal.

For one week survey your thoughts five times a day. Have you been dwelling on the negative or the positive? Have you been throwing yourself a pity party, or have you been expressing gratitude? Have you been thinking the best about yourself and others or the worst? Have you been thinking about all that's wrong with your world or all that's right with Christ? In other words, stop and consider what is capturing your thoughts. Your focus journal will provide good insight as to how biblical your perspective really is. Beyond that, do the following:

- Do more with less. Instead of reading the Bible for fifteen minutes straight, read three to five verses and spend the remaining time meditating on those verses. Memorize them, say them out loud, think through each part, and practice meditation.
- Each day during your time with the Lord, pray Ephesians 1:17–19 over your life and ask the Holy Spirit to reveal the Bible in a fresh and new way.
- If there are conflicts in any of your relationships, ask yourself, "How can I seek better understanding in this relationship? How can I resolve conflict in a peaceful way? And how can I extend grace to others I have difficulty with?"

We cannot conclude this devotional reading without dealing with our perspective on the lost and unchurched. Jesus addressed this perspective with the disciples in John 4:35 when he said, "Open your eyes and look at the fields, they are ripe for harvest." Do I really see spiritually seeking people as ready to take a step toward Christ?

When it comes to reaching others, a faulty perception often binds us. We assume they will never want Jesus, will laugh at us if we try to share Christ with them, or will roll their eyes when we invite them to church. This is simply not always true. In fact, according to author Thom Rainer, 82 percent of the unchurched are at least somewhat likely to come to church if a friend invites them.[2] Those are pretty good odds! We must see them as Christ sees them, as harassed and helpless, like sheep without a shepherd, who need a friend to steer them toward God's love (Matt. 9:36). We must make the same decision about the lost Paul made in 2 Corinthians 5:16. "No longer do we regard them from a worldly point of view."

In other words they are either lost or found. How we see them could mean all the difference in whether we tell them about Jesus. Our perspective could have a direct impact on where they spend eternity.

How about You?

1. Do you have a biblical perspective of God, yourself, and others? In what ways could this perspective be strengthened?

2. What discipline are you the strongest in, and in which are you the weakest (meditation, revelation, information, or application)? What steps can you take to strengthen these disciplines?

3. Do you really see the unchurched the way God sees them? What difference does our perspective make when it comes to reaching those who don't know Christ as their Savior?

Day 3: The Power of Prayer—Crying Out (Simeon)

Yesterday we talked about developing biblical perception in our lives. This was the first stage of the journey toward Leah's freedom and is found in the name of her first child, Reuben, whose name means "see, a son" and also sounds like the Hebrew for "he has seen my misery." Today we are going to look at biblical prayer from the second stage in her journey with the birth of her second son, Simeon, whose name means "one who hears." Not only did God see Leah, but he also heard her. I have a feeling the prayers she prayed weren't common to the average Christian.

The prayers Leah likely prayed out loud, along with the prayers of David, Job, and many other men and women throughout the Bible, were not the same kind of prayers you and I tend to pray today. We have a habit of sugarcoating our prayers and making them sound spiritual. We can fall into the trap of thinking we should sanitize our prayers to the point that we sound spiritual or at least try to sound spiritual. Too many Christians cover up their emotions and bottle their pain when they come to prayer. We misinterpret the concept of reverence to thinking God won't tolerate our being brutally honest with him. I like the way Hannah Moore expresses the need for honest prayer. "Prayer is not eloquence, but earnestness; not the definition of helplessness, but the feeling of it; not figures of speech, but earnestness of soul."

Why are we hesitant to become gut-level honest with God about our lives? Is it because we fear what he may think of us? Not Leah and not those who experience a deep and desperate need for God to do lasting works in their lives. We must not be afraid of telling God just how we feel. And we must learn biblical prayer in the middle of life's struggles. It begins with crying out to God.

Crying Out

We seldom think of prayer as "crying out." However, crying out is a form of biblical prayer and is found throughout Scripture. The Bible calls this crying out "lament prayers." Remember the Old Testament book of Lamentations, written by Jeremiah, the weeping prophet who cried out to God for his untreatable wound and pain? Prayers of crying out to God are prayers to God in times of need, sickness, affliction, trial, pain, sorrow, or crisis.

In a way Leah would understand, our lives aren't all joy, happiness, and strength. At times we experience exactly the opposite. If praise is a spontaneous response to happiness in life, lamentation is a spontaneous response to pain. If praise is a "Wow!" then lamentation is an "Ouch!"

The reasons for our crying out can come from pain—physical, emotional, mental, or spiritual—or from a delay in seeing our pain being dealt with. I've also seen and experienced crying out when our prayer was unanswered. This can lead to feeling like God is abandoning us and, if we aren't careful, can lead to doubting his goodness in our lives. We must cry out and believe he hears us and will answer us in his timing and way.

Consider the following from the book of Psalms:

- Psalm 3:4—"To the Lord I cry aloud, and he answers me from his holy hill."
- Psalm 34:17—"The righteous cry out, and the Lord hears them; he delivers them from all their troubles."
- Psalm 88:1–2—"O Lord, the God who saves me, day and night I cry out before you. May my prayer come before you; turn your ear to my cry."
- Psalm 118:5—"In my anguish I cried out to the Lord, and he answered me by setting me free."

To cry out means to pray the raw and real emotions that come from sincere honesty. It can mean lifting up a loud voice to the Lord, shouting to him in desperation, and allowing tears to fall from your face as they naturally come. It is simply unhindered and uninhibited prayer. Leah discovered that God hears and answers such prayers. The Bible is filled with examples of God's answering the cries of his children.

- Elijah cried out, and God revived a dead child (1 Kings 17:20–22).
- Jehoshaphat cried out, and God delivered him from death (2 Chron. 18:31).
- Hezekiah cried out, and God gave him victory (2 Chron. 32:2–21).
- Blind Bartimaeus cried out to Jesus, and Jesus restored his sight (Mark 10:46).
- Jesus's disciples cried out to him in a storm, and Jesus calmed the sea (Luke 8:23–24).

Just as a good, earthly dad is quick to answer the cry of his child, Psalm 34:18 says, "The Lord is close to the broken hearted and saves those who are crushed in spirit." God promised us in Psalm 50:15, "Call upon me in the day of trouble and I will deliver you." He promises to answer when we cry out, but we must do so with genuine humility.

At women's church camp there was often a team-building game called the "Blind Maze." The women were blindfolded and led to a rope maze, where they were told to follow the rope until they reached the exit. They were repeatedly told that if they needed help, they should stop and raise their hands; someone would come. Round and round the women went, passing the same tree, going around each other with no exit to be found. One by one they raised their hands, only to have the one in charge whisper to take off the blindfold and move to a spot to watch others. Tears came to their eyes as they watched women continue to go around and around; they knew others were asking for help but not those still in the maze. They could seemingly do the maze on their own. The only way out was to stop and admit they needed help.[1]

I cannot tell you how many times I've cried out to the Lord, and the punch line is ultimately, "God I need you!" I've learned that these four words mean everything when it comes to moving up to the next level in any area of life.

We often advise others to achieve the next level through instilling new disciplines, executing better leadership, or networking strategically.

Though these levels are valuable and even biblical, they aren't the starting point of "moving up." James tells us in 4:10, "Humble yourselves before the Lord, and he will lift you up." Humility, honesty, and even brutal transparency with God are often the true starting points for lasting change. We move up by first moving down to our knees in true humility.

Crying out not only expresses humility; it also states our helplessness without him. Jesus said, "Without me you can do nothing" (John 15:5). This fact is never more a reality than when we are at our wits' end.

I once heard it said, "My ending is God's beginning." When I come to the end of my strength and cry out in desperation to God, it is then that I experience an infusion of his power and might to endure difficulties. Scripture says, "He opposes the proud, but gives grace to the humble" (James 4:6). This grace becomes God's enabling power that I need—to do whatever it takes to rise to the next level.

What's important to note is that crying out to God often leads to praying with expressed trust in the Lord. Pastor Toby Powers tells the story of a heart-broken little girl who knelt and poured out her heart to God at the altar of her local church. She didn't know what to say. As she wept speechlessly, she began to remember what her father had told her. "God knows your needs even before you pray, and he can answer when you don't even know for what to ask." So she began to say her alphabet. A concerned adult from that church knelt beside her and heard her sobbing and saying her ABCs; the adult inquired as to what exactly she was trying to do. The little girl said, "I'm praying to God from my heart."

The adult answered, "It sounds to me more like you're saying the alphabet!"

"Yes," she said, "but God knows more about what I need than I do, and he can take all these letters and arrange them in just the right way to hear and answer my prayers!"[2]

Nearly every prayer of transparency David prayed in the book of Psalms transitioned with a huge "but." As you read his psalms, you feel the emotion pouring out of his heart to God. At points of exhaustion, David would accuse God of leaving him and being the sole source of his desperate situation. His crying out would transition into a "but," and he would begin to exalt the character and nature of God. For example, Psalm 13 is worth reading in full.

> How long, O Lord? Will you forget me forever? How long will you hide your face from me? How long must I wrestle with my thoughts and every day have sorrow in my heart? How long will my enemy triumph over me? Look on me and answer me, O Lord my God. Give light to my eyes, or I will sleep in death; my enemy will say, "I have overcome him," and my foes will rejoice when I fall. But I trust in your unfailing love, my heart rejoices in your salvation. I will sing to the Lord, for he has been good to me.

David exercised brutal transparency with God by asking honest questions. His hurt became hope, however, when he expressed trust in the Lord. He did so by first rejoicing in his salvation.

When it seems like you have nothing to praise God for, you actually have everything to praise God for—your salvation! Next, David remembered that God had been faithful to him in the past by summing up his journey with God in a statement we can all make: "He has been good to me." The psalmist disclosed that even though he had been complaining to God, he hadn't lost his faith in him. Remembering his faithfulness in the past will give birth to the faith I will need in my present. I can then have the courage to face my circumstances and the confidence to do whatever is necessary to move on.

Moving On

Exodus 14:15 has always been a powerful verse of Scripture for me personally. God was leading his people out of Egypt, and Pharaoh was in hot pursuit, unwilling to make this an easy journey of deliverance for God's people. In fact, Pharaoh's dealing with God's people as they were in bondage depicts what I described in yesterday's reading: the battle of "remaining just as we are."

Pharaoh changed his mind several times, and even after enduring ten plagues, he now regretted his decision to let them go. The Egyptian army was ready to pounce on this defenseless prey with no obvious options for escape, because the Israelites were cornered by a mountain range on one side, the Egyptians on the other side, and the Red Sea directly in front of them. It was in this place of life, death, and despair that they cried out to God. God said something powerful to Moses: "Why are you crying out to me? Tell the Israelites to move on." In other words, there is a time to stop crying and start moving. And as they stepped out in faith, the Red Sea parted, and they were able to pass through on dry ground, while the sea swallowed their enemies alive.

The point of crying out to God isn't to remain in that place but to receive, as Hebrews 4:16 says, mercy and grace to help us in our time of need. This mercy and grace help us move beyond where we've been and possess our rightful place of wholeness in Christ. Sharing our deepest thoughts and struggles with God binds us to him and brings his healing to our spirits. Though we might cry out several times along the way, there will always come a whisper from heaven: "I've seen you. I've heard you. I've strengthened you. Now move on."

This was the critical place Leah came to in our story. She grew in the understanding of biblical perspective and biblical prayer, but now she needed to grow in the understanding of how to move on and break unhealthy emotional patterns in her life. She cried out and made the decision to move out. This will be the subject of our reading tomorrow.

How about You?

1. Do you feel like you've every truly cried out to God? What misconceptions about prayer have prevented you from doing this? Do you really believe God is big enough to handle your deepest heart cry? Do you feel safe enough with God to truly express to him how you're feeling at any given moment?

2. Today we looked at expressing transparency and trust as part of our prayer lives. What are five things God has specifically done for you that you can always recall from your past to build your faith today?

3. Whether you've ever felt a need to call out to God before with the same desperation as Leah, the unchurched are always "worth" crying out to God. Are you truly praying—in fact, praying hard—for your one unchurched friend during this 1–2–3 Challenge?

Day 4: The Power of Principles—Attachment Issues (Levi)

After giving birth to her third son, Leah said, "'Now at last my husband will become attached to me, because I have borne him three sons.' So he was named Levi" (Gen. 29:34). Leah had adopted a new strategy to win Jacob's attention and love; she wanted him to become attached to her. Attachment is defined as the affectional tie between husband and wife.

You can hear the desperation in Leah when you read this verse. She tried to compete for her husband's love and affection through childbearing but saw no signs of improvement in their relationship. Jacob was no more attached to her with three sons than he was with one. It's unfair to look deep into these verses and assess Leah's every thought and action, but even after having Reuben (and learning about a God who sees her) and having Simeon (and discovering a God who hears her), it appears that Leah was still circling around her emotional baggage.

We too persist in battling our baggage, even after learning lessons that should have liberated us. We are believers in progress, and I'm thankful for God's grace, but there comes a time when the work of the Holy Spirit must finally sink deep enough into your spirit to make a permanent difference. We must not get the idea that the work of the Holy Spirit is done in a flash of lightning, like a microwaveable dinner. The deep work of the Holy Spirit progresses at the pace at which we willingly cooperate. When we murmur and complain, like the children of Israel in the wilderness, the pace slows to a crawl. When we cooperate with the work of God in our lives, even though it involves struggle and possible pain, we become aware of the steady progression to higher levels and freedom. This is what happened with Leah.

Leah learned through life's struggles that if God saw and heard her, then he would also become her complete source of wholeness for her life. She could stop looking for love in empty wells and find her sense of self-worth in the Lord. Only he could truly satisfy her deepest longings.

The same is true for us. Finding the affirmation of others, having a sense of purpose and possessing a dream, and even enjoying hobbies and interests can satisfy us on some level. But on our deepest level these wells run dry, are unpredictable at best, will fill us one day, and leave us bone dry the next; but Jesus will never do that. This is why he calls himself the "living water" in John 4:14. "But whoever drinks the water I give them will never thirst again." I love the commentary Greg Laurie provides on this verse.

> If you drink from the well of success, you will thirst again. If you drink from the well of accomplishments, you will thirst again. If you drink from the well of experiences, you will thirst again. Whatever it is, it will leave you empty.
>
> Maybe you have tried to satisfy your spiritual thirst with the things this world has to offer and haven't found the satisfaction you're looking for. You didn't find it in that relationship. You didn't find it in that object. You didn't even find it in religious activities. The only place you will find it is in Jesus Christ.
>
> Are you spiritually thirsty today? Christ can satisfy your deepest thirst.[1]

Drinking from the wrong well was a pattern Leah had to break to find the sense of self-worth only God could provide. She tried to attach herself to Jacob through childbearing but came to the revelation that she needed to detach herself from unhealthy emotional patterns. We must also detach ourselves from unhealthy patterns by attaching ourselves to healthy disciplines found in God's word.

Establishing Godly Patterns

Romans 12:1–2 says, "Therefore, I urge you, brothers, in view of God's mercy, to offer your bodies as living sacrifices, holy and pleasing to God; this is your spiritual act of worship. Don't conform any longer to the patterns of this world, but be transformed by the renewing of your mind."

I first and foremost must drink the living water we've just talked about by having meaningful time in God's presence each day. There is nothing that strengthens me, comforts me, convicts me, encourages me, helps me, and sustains me like experiencing God's presence. Whether it is an hour with God each morning, fifteen minutes with him on the way to work, or ten minutes during my break time, I must establish some kind of pattern of experiencing God every day.

Living out Scripture is impossible without experiencing the presence of God, embracing the right motive when it comes to change, and then instilling disciplined principles in our lives. It is an inside-out process, beginning with a work of God in our hearts, so that eventually we walk out with our feet. This process rises and falls on the presence of God and the activity of the Holy Spirit in my life.

Jesus said in John 15:5, "I am the vine, you are the branches. If you remain in me and I in you, you will bear much fruit; *apart from me you can do nothing*" (emphasis added). I must come to a place of dependence on the Lord, realizing I can do nothing without him. Bearing spiritual fruit in my life will be one of the results of dependence on the Lord. As surely as a tree is dependent on water to produce good fruit, dependence is the vital ingredient for our lives to become fruitful for the kingdom of God. We become like those we spend the most time with, and when I remain close to him, I take on his character, and his presence strengthens me to live out godly patterns in my life.

Daily time in his presence serves as the catalyst for the renewing of my mind, which according to Romans 12:2 is the primary way my life is transformed. I have discovered that spending the first fifteen minutes of my day in his presence can establish a Christ-centered mind-set for the rest of the day. My time with him gives me something to always refer back to and reflect on should I become stressed, tempted, or overwhelmed. Colossians 3:2 tells us to set our minds on the things above and not on the things below. Paul tells us in Philippians 4:8, "Finally, brothers, whatever is true, whatever is noble, whatever is right, whatever is pure, whatever is lovely, whatever is admirable, if anything is excellent or praiseworthy, think about such things." It is simply impossible to fulfill these two verses without instituting a pattern of daily devotion in our lives.

If you're just beginning a journey with Christ or realize your need to spend time with God daily but are just not sure how, following the SOAP Bible study technique is something I have followed for years and still recommended to new and seasoned Christians alike.

When it comes to prayer time, I might pray about several things, but I also have a specific prayer focus for each day. On Mondays I pray for my family. On Tuesdays I pray for the staff and students in my school of missions. On Wednesdays I pray for the event where I am ministering over the weekend. On Thursdays I pray for the lost. On Fridays I pray for whatever comes to my heart, or I usually just spend that time in praise and worship. My weekend prayer life usually revolves around my schedule of ministry.

This is my pattern. It keeps me focused each day in my quiet times and assures me that I am going to experience his presence daily. What is your Bible reading plan and the prayer pattern you follow each day to ensure connection to his presence?

Remember, "Therefore" Is Your Turning Point

The second way to experience God's daily presence is found in the first word of Romans 12. "*Therefore*, I urge you, brothers, in view of God's mercy" (emphasis added). I once heard it said that when you see "therefore" in the Bible, you should find out what it's "there for." And as it turns out, it's there for a tremendous reason.

Paul was almost finished writing Romans, his trademark letter of the New Testament. He spent eleven chapters focusing on the vastness of God's grace, mercy, and wisdom expressed in redeeming mankind.

Then he transitioned to five chapters concerning our conduct. It began with chapter 12, starting out with, "Therefore, *in view of God's mercy*, present your bodies as living sacrifices" (emphasis added). Paul said we must behave based on who God is and on what he has done for us.

This message seems a little lopsided, doesn't it? We find eleven chapters about God's character and our belief and only five chapters about our conduct and behavior. We tend to reverse the order and say the gauge of successful Christianity is how well we behave, not on how well we believe. But Paul understood that unless the backdrop of our faith was rooted in the understanding of God's grace, our motive for obedience would be rooted in external duties, not internal devotion to the Lord.

Let me drive home this point just a little more. When I was in middle school, our eighth-grade class put on a play. They needed an extra stagehand and asked me to fill in. I had no idea what I was getting myself into. All I heard was, "Move this, arrange that, get this prop ready, make sure this actor has his costume," etc., etc., etc.! The role was frantic, to say the least, and something I decided never to do again. I laid my head down the night after the first showing and realized something that would frustrate me even more. The audience never saw the hard work of the stagehands. They never saw what was happening backstage to make the production on the front of the stage seem so easy. But it was the *unseen* that made everything *seen* so successful.

The same is true for us. I have expounded on the concept of perceptions and beliefs in this week's reading, but they are the necessary materials that comprise the backstage of our lives. Our unseen beliefs can determine our seen behavior, and the Holy Spirit, our counselor, is the great stagehand who is at work within us to will and act according to his good purpose (Phil. 2:13).

If I understand who Christ is in me and who I am in him, then behaving correctly becomes far easier. And with his grace as the backdrop to my faith, Scripture says it teaches me to say no to ungodliness and becomes the reason I want to honor him (Titus 2:12).

Now look once again at the life of Leah, and you will see this principle playing out. Remember, she had three children whose names revealed different aspects of God's character. Before her final breakthrough, God could have easily said to her, "Therefore, in light of you knowing me as a God who sees you, hears you, and completes you, now embrace my pattern for your life!" And the same is true for us. In light of his mercy and all he has done to call me his child, I will no longer desire to conform to any pattern of this world. And through a close relationship with the living water, I will receive the strength to discipline myself to conform to God's patterns for my life. I will desire to give the great offering.

Concluding with the Greatest Offering

Paul told us that, in light of God's great mercy, to offer our bodies as living sacrifices. In other words, set yourself apart as life worship to God. This is greater than any offering of food to the needy, clothes to the poor, or money to the church. Paul said the standard of worship is that Christ gets our entire lives and nothing less. That is our greatest offering. In fact, to be a Christian means we are the temple of the Holy Spirit and should worship the God of heaven with our entire lives on this earth.

I love Proverbs 4:23, because the general framework for all godly patterns is found in this verse. "Above all else, guard your heart for it is the wellspring of life. Put away perversity from your mouth; keep corrupt talk far from your lips. Let your eyes look straight ahead, fix your gaze directly before you. Make level paths for your feet and take only ways that are firm. Do not swerve to the right or the left, keep your foot from evil."

- My heart—David said, "May the words of my mouth and the meditations of my heart, be pleasing in your sight" (Psalm 19:14). What am I dwelling on the most? Do I take my thoughts captive, or do I allow my mind to wander into worldly thinking? How am I really doing when it comes to areas such as bitterness, anger, lust, envy, criticism, and other sins that find their breeding ground in the mind?
- My mouth—This is a tough one. Am I taming my tongue? Am I avoiding unwholesome talk? Am I critical or complimentary? Generally speaking, do I honor God with my mouth?
- My eyes—Scripture tells us to avoid the appearance of evil and to come out from the world and be separate. What am I watching on TV, listening to on the radio, and looking at online?
- My feet—Am I taking ways that are firm? Meaning, do I take the high road in the affairs of my life? Do I live with honor and integrity? Am I an honest person?

To guard our hearts means to guard the very presence of God in our lives by walking in these godly patterns. Leah experienced a greater awareness of his presence as unhealthy patterns were broken and godly patterns were established. The same will be true for us. As I offer the parts of my body to Christ, the awareness of his presence and the many blessings we experience will become deeper and richer in our lives.

How about You?

1. Write out your pattern of seeking the Lord on a daily basis. What Bible study method do you use? What will be your prayer focus for each day of the week?

2. Is your motive to change and follow through on your hinge decision ultimately rooted in God's great grace and in what he has done for you? What tends to serve as the primary backdrop of your walk with Christ? Grace or legalism? Faith or fear?

3. Read through Proverbs 4:23 again. Which area of your life do you need to offer to the Lord again? When was the last time you committed your body and your entire life to him?

Day 5: The Power of Praise—"This Time" Must Become "All The Time"! (Judah)

The goal of our "this time" decision is to become our "all the time" reality. God desires to take us to higher heights and for us to remain in a place of newfound freedom. Though Leah would have more children through her maidservants, after the four we talked about in this week's reading, the Scripture says in Genesis 28:35, "Then she stopped having children." She stopped having children after giving birth to Judah, whose name means "praise."

After giving birth to "praise," I believe Leah achieved a level of freedom she had never experienced before, because she reached a measure of growth where "this time" started becoming "all the time." She reached what has been called "a pregnant pause," where the work of God would become deeper and grow to a permanent level over time.

Some of you have already read ahead in your Bible and have noticed that Leah appears to still compete with Rachel on some level. And I agree. However, "some level" isn't the same as the "same level." There was definite growth in her life, and she achieved a permanent measure of freedom. I'm not suggesting that her life and family struggles fell away like ripe fruit from a tree, but I'm suggesting that she had a newfound freedom in dealing with those struggles. Allow me to illustrate.

When I was in college, one of my part-time jobs was cleaning out apartments of departed college students who'd lived in the apartment complexes around the university. We called this day "trash out." Our job was simple: Go into each apartment and see what trash the college students had left behind. Then bag up, load up, and clean out the major trash still in the apartment. We kept a list of how many bags and items came from those apartments, and those loads of trash were then subtracted from the deposit owed to the tenant. Each apartment we opened was a complete surprise. You held your breath, crossed your fingers, whispered a prayer, and opened the door to see what had been left behind. Hopefully it was a little amount, but more times than not, each apartment required a significant amount of "trash out."

Not to sound degrading at all, but you could say that Leah's life, just like some of those apartments, required a bit of work. But the most rewarding part of "trash out" was walking through the apartment complex at the end of the fifteen-hour workday and opening each door again to make sure we had collected everything. The results compared to the start of the day were very rewarding. However, the reason for the hurry was because the deep-cleaning ladies, carpet guys, and painters would always come the next day to make the apartment look brand new.

Leah's life after the birth of Judah was comparable to when we opened the door to check each apartment for the second time. There was a major difference from the first time we'd laid eyes on it, but there was still obvious work to be done. However, the fun part was about to begin as highly skilled craftsmen were getting ready to do their magic. Our job was to get the old stuff out so they could get the new stuff in.

The same could be said about the process of freedom Leah experienced in her life. Before the birth of "praise" in her life, major stuff was being removed, namely false perceptions and past hurts. But as God does with us, he doesn't stop with "trash out." He finishes with "truth in." Truth from God's word and truth from the great counselor, the Holy Spirit, will continue to make us new. And so today, let's not focus on "trash out" but on the truth God instills in us to help "this time" become "all the time."

Let's look at three truths God wants to instill in our lives as he, the expert craftsman, moves in the new stuff and makes our lives ready for even greater use by him. Let's explore three ways God makes "this time" into "all the time."

God Uses My Pain to Birth a Great Sense of Purpose in My Life

One truth about our pain is that God can use it to birth a great sense of purpose in our lives. By doing so, "this time" becomes "all the time." With our pain in his hand and with a desire for God to do something significant with our lives, there's no stopping what God can do in and through our lives. Not only that, but I've often noticed that people achieve a greater level of freedom from their struggles when they use that struggle as a platform to help others. It's as if they give out of their brokenness to others who are hurting, and God is able to deepen the levels of healing in their own lives.

A great couple who exemplify this truth are Jason and Cindy Gaskins. I first met them at a baseball park, and after shaking hands, someone said to me, "That's the Jay's Hope lady."

I said, "The who?"

It turns out Cindy started a foundation in our city to help support families with children battling cancer. When I asked what had motivated her to do so, I was told about Jay, her four-year-old son, who died of cancer. Hence the ministry of Jay's Hope was born from their loss. Now, this couple has served hundreds—maybe thousands!—of parents by providing hands-on help and educational material for families with children battling cancer. From their hurt, hope was born, and if you asked Cindy today, she would tell you that helping others has assisted to further her own healing.

I distinctly remember my youth pastor, Joe, telling a story after I received Christ at the age of eighteen. I can't remember any names or many of the details, but the punch line has stuck with me to this day. There was a little old lady in the community, connected to the church, who battled depression. Joe went on to say that the way this lady battled her depression was by finding others who were depressed and encouraging them. That's powerful! That's making a decision not to allow a struggle to define you and for you to define your struggle. God uses our pain to bring purpose into our lives, and as we embrace this purpose, further healing is accomplished in our hearts. The trash is kept out, and continuous truth that keeps us free floods in. This truth gives us a "but" at the end of every prayer.

The Big "But"

David ended prayers of lament with a "but." He poured his heart out to God in brutal honesty, then pivoted his prayers with a "but" about God's character. Time and time again, he essentially said, "God, I am suffering, *but* I trust that you are faithful." Proclaiming God's character as you pray elevates your faith above your feelings and gives you a biblical perspective on your situation. However, let's take this exercise to another level. Let's pray the word of God.

When I first became a Christian, Dee Dee Stephens, who led me to the Lord, mailed me a book about thirty days after I'd committed my heart to the Lord. It was a book entitled *Prayers That Avail Much for Teens*. I opened the small book, and there on the inside of the front cover she had written an encouraging note that concluded with, "Always remember to pray the Word of God." Being a new Christian and not exactly knowing the "best" way to pray, I devoured that little book from cover to cover, doing exactly what she'd said and praying the prayers out loud in my quiet times.

Every line in that little book was actually a Bible verse in the format of a prayer. Two things hit me like a ton of bricks. First, praying the word of God is powerful because it exalts the authority of God over my life and circumstances. And second, I discovered I couldn't pray the word of God out loud without my prayer time turning into worship. Jesus said, "The words I speak to you are Spirit and they are life." As I prayed the word, I was praying life, and life always has a sense of celebration and worship connected to it. I encourage you with the words of Dee Dee Stephens. In some way, always pray the word.

Finally, Remember That Your Scars Point People to a Bigger Story

Speaking of celebration, I will never forget the girl who came to me at youth camp with tears streaming down her face as she giggled almost uncontrollably. I asked her whether everything was OK. She busted out with, "Everything is more than great." As it turns out, this girl was a cutter, who literally took razor blades to her arms and legs. Cutting has become an epidemic in today's younger generation, and as another teenager once said to me, "I cut so the pain I feel on the outside helps me to forget the pain I feel on the inside." Talk about a gut-wrenching battle! But for this particular young lady at the youth camp, something had shifted for her that night in the service. "This time" was about to become "all the time." You could sense it. As she shared her story, with fresh scars on her arms, she said something that to this day has remained with me. "I realized tonight that Jesus bled so I don't have to!" Wow! Her words still give me goose bumps all these years later.

This young lady, with the help of the Holy Spirit, did what we must do with those areas of pain in our lives. We must connect our struggle to his story and allow his story to win in our lives. And when we do, our scars start pointing to his great story. This young lady probably still has some scars, but when she looks at them, she doesn't remember a razor blade; she remembers the cross. She doesn't remember her blood. She now remembers his. And now, as others ask her about her scars or she reveals them to those who are hurting, she can point to a Savior who bled so she no longer has to. He took on her pain and gave her a tremendous story to share with others.

Conclusion

There are two things I would like for us to come away with from this week's reading. First, healing, wholeness, and freedom take time. I've heard it said that God asks us to strive for progress as he makes perfect the work he starts in our lives. And I agree.

Second, I want us to feel a breath of fresh air. Just as I walked into some of those apartments that were once full of trash and were being prepared to be made new, God will do the same for you and me. He will engage in "trash out" and "truth in" to finish every good work he has started in our lives (Phil. 1:6). Be encouraged that "this time" can and will become "all the time."

How about You?

1. Where do you find yourself in the "trash out" and "truth in" process? Do you still feel as though there is much to be removed, or do you feel as though it is the season of the truth coming in? Do you believe God can do this work simultaneously in your life? If so, what is the one thing he is taking out and one truth he is trying to put into your life?

2. Who is one person in your life you can encourage? You may not have a Jay's Hope kind of story, but you can remember the little old lady. She dealt with her depression by finding someone depressed and encouraging him or her. How can you apply this principle to your biggest struggle?

3. What story do your scars tell? In other words, how has the story of Christ intersected with the story behind your scars? How can you use your story to point others to the story of Christ?

CHAPTER 4:

WEEK 4—MY DEPENDENCE

Day 1: Jacob's Lean

This week marks the halfway point through *A Life That Wins,* the halfway point to your hinge decision, and the halfway point for those of you participating in Reach the City. It is an important week, because at the halfway point of any kind of spiritual commitment you make, fatigue can settle in, the enemy can come against you, and you can either choose to backpedal on your hinge decision or allow it to become permanent in our life. But my prayer for you is that the Holy Spirit will energize you at this halfway point, that you will become stronger and not weaker in your hinge decision, and that you will gain a new sense of determination to finish this forty-day commitment strong.

This can happen only as we learn our fourth winning principle, dependence on the Lord. By now you have probably discovered more than ever your need to depend on God—not only to complete this challenge but also to live a victorious life in general. We simply need God's strength and his help in the details of our daily lives. The temptation we all face, however, is to try to do things in our own strength, to take matters into our own hands, and to control circumstances and situations we should simply trust to the Lord. I think we can all agree that this effort on our part doesn't usually end very well. The individual in the Bible who best portrays the pitfalls of independence and the pathway to biblical dependence is Jacob from the Old Testament.

Jacob's story is found in Genesis 25:19–33. His name means "supplanter, deceiver, and heel grasper."[1] He was given this name at birth because he literally grasped the heel of his twin brother, Esau, as they were being born. What a baby picture that would have been, but it became a prophetic picture of Jacob's character over the course of his life. Figuratively speaking, he learned to cause others, namely Esau, to trip up and stumble for his own personal gain. With the help of his mother, Rebekah, he took advantage of Esau, played on his weaknesses, and pressured him to exchange the rights of the firstborn for a bowl of soup.

This act was foolishness on Esau's part, but the cunning plan worked. Next, he and Rebecca lied to Isaac so Jacob could receive the blessing of the firstborn—which also belonged to Esau. At this point Esau was outraged, and Jacob was found fleeing to his Uncle Laban's home for safety. After receiving a powerful dream from God on his way there, he remained with Laban for more than twenty years.

He then fell into the same trap of self-sufficiency and shrewd behavior, fled back to his homeland, had another powerful spiritual encounter, and then finally reconciled with Esau.

This is a loaded story full of some deep spiritual truths, but if we aren't careful, we can miss the most powerful one of all because it was actually revealed before Jacob was born. In Genesis 25:21–23, we are told that Rebekah was barren and that Isaac prayed to the Lord on her behalf. The Lord answered his prayer, and she became pregnant with twin boys. Verse 22 tells us the boys jostled within her, and when she prayed about the matter, she received a great promise from God in the next verse: "Two nations are in your womb, and two peoples from within you will be separated; one people will be stronger than the other, and the older will serve the younger." God actually promised Jacob's call to leadership before he was even born. Why in the world, then, did this great promise turn into a dreadful plot of manipulation and deceit? When we study the story closely, we find that a doubting mother, a declining father, a deceiving son, and the godless desires of a brother all contributed to one of the greatest stories of duplicity in the entire Bible.

Jacob's Lean Was a Family Thing

Rebekah and Isaac were married for twenty years before having twin boys. They received a powerful promise from God concerning Jacob, but many people don't realize that Jacob was seventy-seven years old when he and his mother deceived Esau. That means after waiting twenty years for children, Rebekah then waited for another seventy-seven years, wondering how in the world God's promise would come to pass. Certainly time took its toll on Rebekah's faith, and she began to doubt. This doubting has happened to the best of us. We can easily begin to lean on our own understanding and take matters into our own hands.

Next to John 3:16, Proverbs 3:5–6 is probably the passage most Christians have memorized. 'Trust in the Lord with all your heart and lean not on your own understanding. In all your ways acknowledge him, and he will make your paths straight." This verse resonates deeply with our human tendency to start depending on ourselves and leaning on our own understanding when our faith is being tested.

There is no doubt that Rebekah began to doubt and lean on her own understanding. She came up with a deceitful plot to help God fulfill his promise, and Jacob participated willingly in her plan. Instead of going to God in prayer, as she had done years before, she depended on her own plans. Because of her weakness, this habit became Jacob's habit, and she would pay dearly for her sin; she would never see him again. But she wasn't the only party at play in this saga; Isaac was equally guilty. Even though he might appear as a passive victim in a sinful strategy, this was far from reality.

First, he allowed his home to become divided. He loved and preferred Esau, and Rebekah loved Jacob. By choosing to play favorites, they would lose the favor of God needed to fulfill the original promise. Also, when his eyesight became bad, Isaac leaned on his own ability to make things happen rather than waiting on and trusting the Lord. His physical disability started influencing his life more than his faith in God's ability.

This is demonstrated in our story because at the time he urgently requested to bless his firstborn, he appeared as though he was on the verge of death. However, he was 137 years old at that time and lived to be 180! Isaac almost seemed desperate to bless his favorite son, Esau, even though he most certainly knew the promise God had spoken over

Jacob before the twins were born. It is almost as though Isaac forgot God's promise and ability to provide.

His behavior is entirely contrary to the Isaac we first read about in Genesis 22, when God asked his father, Abram, to sacrifice him as a test. He believed his earthly father's words that God would provide a sacrifice even though his life was on the line. And that is exactly what happened. Now, years later, he was choosing to act opposite God's spoken promise to him, being driven by the senses of feeling, eating, and smelling, or living in a state of disbelief. When the faith of a father declines, this lapse can jeopardize the destiny of a family.

Lastly, just as Isaac, Rebekah, and Jacob are worth mentioning, so is Esau. Here is a guy who gave up everything for a bowl of soup. Hebrews 12:16–17 tells us, "See that no one is sexually immoral, or is godless like Esau, who for a single meal sold his inheritance rights as the oldest son. Afterward, as you know, when he wanted to inherit this blessing, he was rejected. He could bring about no change of mind, though he sought the blessing with tears."

More than likely, because his father favored him, he enjoyed the meat of the land and had a tendency to rely on what could be touched and felt. This weakness was magnified in the life of Esau. And it was magnified so much that he gave up his entire inheritance for a single meal. He claimed that he was starving and would die, but the truth is, he just couldn't wait. His flesh was screaming, and he chose to live by his flesh in a critical moment.

We all know the feeling of "just can't wait." It's dangerous because it can cause us to make hasty and poor decisions in the spur of the moment. Thankfully, Esau's story didn't end in total disaster. He forgave his brother after their long separation and apparently learned self-control because he expressed genuine affection for the guy who had taken everything from him twenty years earlier. At any rate Esau's story is a reminder for us to live upright and self-controlled lives, and to choose the desires of the spirit over the desires of our flesh. Even when our flesh is screaming, we must remain faithful.

Conclusion

Certainly Jacob was responsible for his own actions, but we must understand that the atmosphere of his home became a breeding ground for his weaknesses to grow. This is a sobering thought for parents, myself included. The truth is, from one generation to the next, the faith of a mom and dad will become either drastically stronger or significantly weaker over time. Both weaknesses and strengths can be passed from one generation to another. Take, for example, the history of lying in Jacob's family.

Abraham lied about Sarah and told others she was his sister. He did this out of fear, trying to protect the promise of God in his life rather than trusting in the Lord to protect him. Isaac and Rebekah did the same exact thing. And now, in the third generation, Jacob is known as a liar. It isn't a far stretch to say that single acts of deception that seemed innocent in one generation can be characterized in the next. We must understand that a divided home can endanger our children's hearts, and the spiritually passive attitude of a father like Isaac is just as dangerous as intentional acts of sinfulness, as found in the life of Rebekah.

As we look at the life of Jacob this week, we will explore dependence and trust in the Lord. As they relate to our hinge decision, we must learn to depend on the Lord, who is faithful to keep what we entrust to him. Through the life of Jacob, we will learn how God dismantles our strength so that his strength is made perfect in our weaknesses. And as we turn our attention to this week's personal outreach and small group series, we will learn how dependence on the Holy Spirit will help us to effectively reach others. It's going to be a great week.

How about You?

1. We looked at the bigger picture of Jacob's surroundings in today's reading. We looked at the state of his mother and father's faith. What is the current state of your family's faith? As a family, are you growing and becoming stronger in the things of the Lord? As a father, is your faith strengthening or weakening? As a mother, are you living in fear or in faith?

2. When you lean on your own strength, how is this manifested in your life? For example, do you lose sleep worrying about tomorrow? Do you find yourself trying to control others? Do you keep your eyes glued to your bank statements? What, then, are characteristics of those who depend on the Lord?

3. How can you continue to do your part to help strengthen the faith of your family?

Day 2: Jacob's Ladder

Jacob's journey of learning dependence started with his dream in Genesis 28, and it was no small dream. We pick up the scene with Jacob fleeing from his brother. After a hard day of looking over his shoulder for possible signs of Esau, he camped for the night. Without any of his advance knowledge of what was about to happen, God came to Jacob through a dream with powerful promises about his life. This overnight encounter with God gives me cause to marvel at God's goodness. Remember, Jacob was in this predicament because he was a liar and manipulator. If this isn't God's grace at work, I don't know what is.

God doesn't give perfect people dreams; he gives dreams to imperfect people. I believe God knew the journey ahead for Jacob was going to be tough, so he gave him a dream to hold onto during the difficult process ahead. God also knew that at the end of Jacob's journey, both his name and character would change. This tells me that God is a "big picture" God who sees us for who we are now and who we will be in the future. And in this story, God was speaking to Jacob that night, not *as he was*, but as he was *going to be*. This is a great example of God's grace extended to Jacob, and it is the same grace he extends to us today.

The dream had as its visual centerpiece a ladder, of all things. Jacob had tried to climb the ladder of earthly success through manipulative schemes involving his parents. He didn't realize that he was about to embark on a journey where he would discover that true success was first found in the Lord and in the Lord alone. In fact, four powerful truths are revealed in this dream, all of which relate to the principle of dependence in our lives. First, God's leadership in my life, or lack thereof, will determine which way I lean. Second, the true source of blessing is the resource of heaven. Third, powerful promises from God demand his precision. And fourth, I develop dependence by practicing his presence.

The Ladder Determines My Lean

Jacob dreamed about a ladder, and the Bible says in verse 13, "There above it stood the Lord." When you study this account in the Hebrew language, this verse can be translated correctly as either "There above it stood the Lord" or "There beside it stood the Lord." Together, these two translations are a great definition of biblical lordship in our lives.

His lordship should consist of the Lord above us and beside us. He should be both our Lord and our friend, our master and our Father, the one above us and the one beside us.

God had spoken to Rebekah years before concerning the promise of Jacob's life. However, time passed, and Rebekah had either forgotten God's promise or assumed that she would have to make it happen for the promise to be fulfilled. Anytime we try to make God's plan happen and take matters into our own hands, we are dangerously close to tampering with the lordship of Christ in our lives. This was the case for Jacob and Rebekah.

Now Jacob was about to embark on a journey to understand God's lordship in his life. His deceptive character and tendency to lean on himself would be dismantled over time, and he would learn to lean on the Lord as he lived out the journey that awaited him. He would learn what you and I must learn—that life is a walk with the Lord. He should be above us, yes, but he is also beside us every step of the way.

As you study the life of Jacob, it is not too far fetched to speculate that the faith of his father, Isaac, and his grandfather, Abraham, wasn't yet Jacob's own. Jacob didn't seem to have much time for God. We never read in Scripture about any of his conversations about God or with God before Jacob left home.

Jacob had little time for God, because he was too busy scheming and planning how to get ahead. For example, when he lied to his father, Isaac, as he was stealing his brother's birthright, he told him, "The Lord *your* God gave me success" (Gen. 27:20, emphasis added). He wasted too much of his time thinking only of himself.

But God was about to dramatically interrupt his self-centered life.

Jacob had a ways to go before discovering his spiritual identity. He would learn that one marker of spiritual maturity is that we love the God of the dream more than the dream of God. We should love him first as Lord, regardless of the promises we hear around the ladder.

My Source of Blessing Is the Resource of Heaven

Jacob was one of the privileged few who witnessed the workings of the kingdom of God, the spiritual activity of heaven itself. Jacob's ladder is a powerful portrait of prayer and the true source of blessing in a believer's life. Jacob saw angels ascending and descending this heavenly staircase. What a glorious revelation this must have been, and it must have spurred a deep sense of awe in Jacob. Respected theologians believe the ascending and descending angels gave an illustration of the activity in heaven of dispersing the blessings of God. As the angels ascended, they took the prayers of God's people to the throne of heaven. As they descended, they carried the answer of God back to his people.

This is remarkable when you think about it in terms of Jacob's life. He and his mother had executed a deceitful plot to somehow attain the promise of God when all they really needed to do was pray. That sounds so simple, but when our faith is being tested, sometimes the last thing we do is pray. However, it is the very first thing those who are dependent on the Lord do. Abraham Lincoln once said, "I have been driven many times to my knees by the overwhelming conviction that I had nowhere else to go. My own wisdom, and that of all about me, seemed insufficient for the day."

Powerful Promises Require His Precision

Jacob not only saw angels; he heard God speak three powerful promises over his life: "I am with you and will watch over you wherever you go," "I will bring you back to this land," and "I will not leave you until I have done what I promised you." In other words the first promise is, "I will be with you." The second is, "I will watch over you." And the third is, "I will finish what I start!"

The last promise is one of my favorite lines of the entire Old Testament, and it bears repeating. God said to Jacob, "I will not leave you until I have done what I promised." I love this promise. God says, "What I have started, I will finish!" Paul confirmed this promise in Philippians 1:6. "He who began a good work in you is faithful to finish it until the day of Christ Jesus." God was faithful to Jacob, and God is faithful to us. Remember, Hebrews 12:2 says he is the author and *finisher* of our faith.

He finishes what he starts, but we must remember that God takes *his* time when finishing what he starts in our lives. Often the finishing process is all about precision.

My wife and I have built three houses since we became married. My kids were old enough to watch the last one, and they remember the process of a house being built from start to finish. At the beginning of construction with our last home, we told them it would take at least four months from start to finish if the weather cooperated. My kids were shocked at how much progress was initially made in a short amount of time. The foundation was poured, the house was framed, and Sheetrock was hung very quickly. My kids were ecstatic, believing our new home would be completed way ahead of schedule.

From past experience, I knew one thing about building a house—the big stuff doesn't take a great deal of time; it's the little stuff, the attention to detail, that takes the most time. And it did. I remember walking the kids through the house under construction and showing the expertise required to hang the trim, finish the cabinets, and paint every corner of our new home. I remember telling them, "Detail takes time, but without detail we cannot enjoy our home."

The same is true in our relationship with the Lord. Some of the big stuff with God seems to happen almost immediately as a new Christian.

However, he turns his attention toward the details of our character and addresses important factors such as our dependence on him. These works take time, but without them we will never settle in and enjoy the fullness available in Christ, the fullness that comes with maturity as a man or woman of God. His promises require the work of his power in our lives.

Developing Dependence by Practicing His Presence

Jacob woke up from his dream and made a very telling statement in Genesis 28:16. "Surely the Lord was in this place, and I was not aware of it." When he laid his head down to sleep, he didn't realize God was at work in his life. Part of Jacob's journey would consist of God's cultivating a constant awareness of his presence and activity in Jacob's life. God wants to do the same for us. The early church fathers would call this spiritual awareness "God consciousness." It is living in the reality that God is not only with us in a general sense but also always present and working in the intimate details of our lives. Part of the role of the Holy Spirit is to create this God consciousness within us, which is vital to dependence on the Lord.

In the seventeenth century a monk by the name of Brother Lawrence worked in the kitchen of a monastery. This was certainly not a glorious job but one filled with mundane, repetitive activity. Have you ever felt that way in your job? Brother Lawrence decided to make what might appear like a meaningless job meaningful by practicing the presence of God. Throughout the day, he reminded himself of God's presence by shifting his mind to spiritual matters, whispering prayers of gratitude in his heart to God throughout the day, and constantly rejoicing for God's faithfulness with the small things. Brother Lawrence recorded what he had learned through this discipline, and his findings became a best-selling book named after his habit, *The Practice of the Presence of God.* In it, he said,

> A little lifting up of the heart suffices; a little remembrance of God, an interior act of adoration, even though made on the march and with sword in hand, are prayers which, short though they may be, are nevertheless very pleasing to God, and far from making a soldier lose his courage on the most dangerous occasions, bolster it. Let him then think of God as much as possible so that he will gradually become accustomed to this little but holy exercise; no one will notice it and nothing is easier than to repeat often during the day these little acts of interior adoration.[1]

I love how this passage ends with "interior acts of adoration." One of the greatest ways to develop God consciousness and dependency in our lives is by inwardly setting our hearts and minds on things above and not on things below (Col. 3:3). Scripture also tells us in Philippians 4:8 to think about what is pure, noble, excellent, and praiseworthy. This is an inward habit of the heart that is key to abiding in Christ, remaining in him throughout our day, and ultimately bearing much fruit (John 15:5). This is a lifelong discipline to learn, but like Brother Lawrence learned, we have a lifetime to practice God's presence.

Conclusion

Last week we looked at Jacob's lean. His tendency was to lean on his own ability, personality, and craftiness. I have learned that the way we choose to lean is very subtle. Just as a person can shift his or her weight from one leg to another while standing, we can shift our internal weight from ourselves to the Lord throughout our day. We can pause and express interior acts of adoration and whisper prayers of thanksgiving and supplication. On our way to get a drink of water at work, we can think about something we just read in the Bible, and on the way home we can listen to a worship CD and refocus our thoughts on the Lord before greeting our family.

This lean is the way we keep the principles and promises of Jacob's ladder before us always. God is the God above us and the God beside us. He is the one who is with us, will watch over us, and will finish everything he starts. And just as Jacob came to realize that ultimately God is the source of all blessing, we can realize the reality of John 1:16. "From the fullness of his grace, we have all received one blessing after another." Finally, as we look to reach others, we must be aware of God's presence and his activity all around us. Scripture says he isn't willing that any should perish but that all should come to repentance (2 Pet. 3:9).

I believe God is always at work around us in the daily details of our lives, trying to reach someone who hasn't accepted his Son as their savior. We must learn to sense this activity, discern the doors he opens for us to influence others, and walk through them with love. This will be the topic in this week's personal outreach session through your small group.

How about You?

1. Do you live your Christian life understanding that God is both above you and beside you? He is our Lord, the boss of our lives, but also a friend who sticks closer than a brother. Do you tend to live as if one of those attributes is stronger than the other? Is he only a God of rules with little relationship? Or is he maybe all relationship with few rules?

2. Which promise of Jacob is the easiest for you to believe? Which is the hardest?

    - I am with you (the promise of his presence).
    - I will watch over you (the promise of his provision).
    - I will finish what I start (the promise of his fulfilling his promise).

3. Do you think it's impossible in this day and time, amid the flurry of busyness and hectic schedules, to really practice the presence of God and cultivate God consciousness? What are some other ways to develop God dependence in our lives?

Day 3: Jacob's Laban

Welcome to the crucible, also known as Day 24 of *A Life That Wins.* The marine corps "Crucible" is the final test of an eleven-week period of endurance and training for marine recruits. The fires of the Crucible burn away the dross and provide the final passage for young men and women to receive the coveted title of "marine."

The entire test and training are painful and exacting, and they press everyone beyond what he or she thought he or she had to offer; but it is a regimen, a system of purpose. Recruits get eight hours of sleep during the entire fifty-four-hour exercise. They get very little food and are responsible for rationing out the food to themselves. If that weren't enough, the recruits also have to go through tough physical activities like road marches totaling forty miles and night infiltration.

The final march of the Crucible begins at 4:00 a.m. None of the recruits want to drop out at this point, but all of them are tired, weary, and ready to quit. As the sun rises, the recruits cross the DI Bridge. Once they are across, the drill instructors start marching calls, and the recruits join in. As they get closer to the main base, the marching calls get louder, and the recruits grow stronger until they reach the Parade Deck. The recruits form up around a half-size replica of the Marine Corps Memorial—also known as the Iwo Jima Memorial.

A color guard raises the flag on the memorial. The chaplain reads a prayer specifically written for the finish of the Crucible, and the company first sergeant addresses the recruits. Then the drill instructors present each of their recruits with the marine corps insignia—the eagle, globe, and anchor. The instructors shake their hands and call them "marine" for the first time. Many accept the honor with tears streaming down their faces.[1]

The point of military basic training is twofold. The first goal is to teach basic military, combat, and survival skills. The second goal is to push recruits to the end of themselves and squeeze out potential they never realized existed.

God also has a type of basic training for every believer with the same two goals in mind. This was certainly the case for Jacob, but his basic training would last much longer than a marine's eleven weeks. It would last twenty years! It was a process that would teach him fundamentals of the faith that would be key to his future destiny. But at the end his name would be changed, because a different man would emerge from this extended season of basic training.

Most of Jacob's training revolved around his uncle Laban. Whereas we probably don't have an uncle named Laban, we have seasons of life similar to Jacob's that God uses to accomplish the same kind of work in our lives.

For me I have always called this season "the dreaded in-between." It is the time of growth from the man I am to the man I can be. It is a time of trial that God uses to test my faith to ensure it is tried and true. It is a time when I ultimately learn a level of dependence that redefines me to my core. It is a season of hardship in which God changes my heart. It is a season of both internal and external conflict that changes my character forever.

Enduring Hardship as Discipline

Jacob's dream, which we looked at yesterday, started when he laid his head on a rock and fell asleep. This tidbit of information might seem incidental, but it was a prophetic picture because the next two decades of his life would be identified with hardship. For those of you who aren't campers, let me tell you that getting comfortable is hard when a rock is your pillow. You can feel a little sorry for a guy who has been walking all day and needs a good night's sleep. Jacob's night of discomfort, unsettledness, and an overall restlessness was a foretelling of his future years.

Hebrews 12:7-11 gives us a whole new perspective when it comes to how we approach the hardships God uses as our "basic training."

> Endure hardship as discipline; God is treating you as sons. For what son isn't disciplined by his father? If you aren't disciplined (and everyone undergoes discipline), then you are

> illegitimate children and not true sons. Moreover, we have all had human fathers who disciplined us and we respected them for it. How much more should we submit to the Father of our spirits and live! Our fathers disciplined us for a little while as they thought best; but God disciplines us for our good, that we may share in his holiness. No discipline seems pleasant at the time, but painful. Later on, however, it produces a harvest of righteousness and peace for those who have been trained by it.

As I have heard it said, when we face hardships, we can grumble and gripe or choose to grow. Furthermore, we should view these hardships as discipline from the Lord. Usually we shy away from such a perspective because it implies that we've done something wrong and deserve punishment. However, the word *discipline* in the verse above means "the total training of the whole person." God uses hardship to bring wholeness to our lives, and ultimately we see growth in our lives, because he is actually being good to us. Through his time with Laban, Jacob would grow as a servant, understand the law of sowing and reaping, and ultimately come to a place of surrender. And as the writer of Hebrews promised, he would eventually share in God's holiness and find a place of peace.

God's Sovereign Ironies of "In-Between"

Jacob's journey toward peace is full of what I call "sovereign ironies." In everyday life, we use the word *ironic* to mean a circumstance that turns out differently than expected. However, God will sovereignly allow certain events in our lives to teach us dependency and change our character.

For Jacob his years of forced service to Laban for Rachel's hand in marriage were such a circumstance. It was certainly an intentional season from the Lord, which Jacob was learning to serve. Remember, he was used to his own mother serving him, but now Jacob was about to learn hard work and a life of serving others.

Even Jesus would say that he came not to be served but to serve and give his life as a ransom for many. He also told his disciples that whoever wanted to be great must be the least. This type of servant leadership was contrary to Jacob's character but essential to his calling. God used Jacob's time with Laban to teach him a servant's attitude and attentiveness to detail that produces destiny. I have often learned that people who feel called to be a "somebody" will endure a season of feeling like a "nobody" to learn humility and dependence on God. This was certainly true for Jacob.

Not only that, but God also allowed Jacob to develop a work ethic. Work ethic seems to be a rare commodity in today's world but something that must be restored if believers are ever going to walk wholeheartedly in their divine purpose. Laban's school of hard work taught Jacob that even though he could work with his hands, he still needed God's hand on his life for his dream to be fulfilled.

After all, Jacob was comfortable with, and somewhat successful in, scheming his way to success. But to his chagrin, those previously effective skills would be of no effect in the school of "in-between." Through the years Jacob would grow to understand that faith without works is dead but that faith with scheming is unnecessary, ungodly, and ultimately unproductive. No one welcomes this lesson plan from God, but those who don't quit on the purpose of God will cherish the time "in between" for eternity.

Additionally, in our season of in-between, we learn to discern the difference between what we are responsible for and what responsibilities are God's. This process can be very wearisome but certainly worth it in the end.

Jacob's fourteen years of forced service continually involved his reaping much of what he'd sowed in his plot against Esau. Galatians 6:7 tells us, "Don't be deceived, God cannot be mocked. A man reaps what he sows." Jacob didn't just reap from single acts of sinfulness; he reaped from a pattern of sinful behavior rooted in a deceitful character. And so how did God break this pattern? By allowing Jacob to meet his match in Laban. Consider the following:

- At his birth the prophecy was declared over his life that the older would serve the younger. Eventually Esau would serve Jacob, but before this would take place, Jacob would serve Laban.
- He deceived Esau, the firstborn, from his rightful birthright. Now Laban deceived him into marrying his firstborn, Leah.
- Esau was a man of the field who enjoyed the meat of the land. Now Jacob would make a living herding cattle and goats for fourteen years. During those years of hard labor, Laban would deceive him by changing his wages ten times.

God allowed Jacob to meet his deceptive match, not for the fun of watching him squirm, but for Jacob's sake and for us as future readers of Jacob's struggles. Don't overlook the genius of God in this story. He brilliantly weaved the circumstances in which Jacob saw up close the life of a deceiver while allowing Jacob to meet himself: the deceiver, liar, and supplanter. When Jacob looked at Laban, he certainly saw himself, and that wasn't a pretty picture.

Part of what I do is lead a school of missions and outreach for young adults who want to radically grow in their relationship with God and reach people who are without a relationship with Jesus Christ (http:// www. mymissionsjourney.com).1

One thing I have done during orientation for new students is to bring out a full-size mirror and have each one of our journeymen—that's what we call our student missionaries—look at themselves up and down until they become uncomfortable. We have found over the years that few like to stare at themselves in a mirror too long. Given enough time in front of the mirror, most will notice blemishes, imperfections, and points of insecurity.

God in his goodness also pulls out a mirror of the soul for those who want to grow in their relationship with him. The process isn't comfortable because we will be allowed to see the blemishes in our character. In the same way that Adam and Eve were without covering in the Garden, God will gently take away all our cover-ups and facades so we can see our true selves. John Newton might have said it better: "When people are right with God, they are apt to be hard on themselves and easy on other people. But when they aren't right with God, they are easy on themselves and hard on others."

Finally, Jacob not only learned servanthood and the understanding that sowing and reaping would introduce him to the real Jacob; he also came to his first point of surrender through his hardship. As we fast-forward to the end of Jacob's time with Laban, we see that he reverted once more to manipulating events by a cunning scheme to enlarge the size of his flocks before he headed back to his hometown. Jacob could have handled the situation entirely differently in his departure from Laban's home, but he once again chose to take matters into his own hands. Just like the old Herman's Hermits lyric, "Second verse, same as the first," we find Jacob fleeing for his life. Without the quick thinking of Rachel, Jacob would have come to the end of his life at the hand of Laban.

Even though Jacob was unwilling to admit the obvious, his life quickly melted down into a tornado of disaster. This perfect storm of events caused him to come to the end of himself despite the fact that Jacob didn't realize it. But as I've heard it said, the ending of us is the beginning of God. This "rock and a hard place" moment would set up Jacob for his next life-changing encounter with God—an encounter in which he would finally surrender who he was for who he could be. We will look at this further in tomorrow's reading.

Conclusion

The marines endure basic training like no other, a regime that concludes with an experience known as the Crucible. Untapped potential is pulled from deep within the recruits through this grueling process. Upon completing the Crucible, they are given the high honor of being called a marine. Signing up for basic training doesn't yield this honor; only upon finishing training will they hear the officer's pronouncement of their joining the brotherhood of marines.

In the same way there is a reward that awaits us believers. It's ultimately the voice of the heavenly Father saying, "Well done, good and faithful servant." But on this side of heaven, we must endure an initial process, a crucible, if you will. And when we do, we can hear what Jacob heard, a different name bestowed on us when we can hear ourselves say, "I am truly different. I'm a different person. The process was worth it." Again, more on this tomorrow.

Don't minimize the importance of the hinge decision you have committed to the Lord. By keeping your decision, you will give the Lord an opportunity to move you from in-between to the path of purpose and destiny. Take a moment and review the hinge decision you have made and how well you are doing to keep the promise you have made to yourself and God. If you have lacked in being faithful, contact your accountability partner and ask for assistance in getting out of in-between.

How about You?

1. Have you ever felt like you've been in God's crucible? How has your character changed as a result?

2. Who or what has served as your "Laban"? Have you ever endured a season of life in which you met yourself—the real you—and gazed into the "mirror of the soul"? How did you initially respond?

3. God's discipline is for our own good. Do you truly believe God has your best interest at heart as you face hardship? Or do you tend to doubt his goodness when the going gets tough?

Day 4: Jacob's Limp

It was ninth grade, and I was both a competitive soccer player and a cross-country runner. In a moment of great zeal but little wisdom, I had the bright idea to try out for the school's wrestling team to stay in tip-top shape for soccer. Long story short, it killed me. I could run miles without stopping, but five minutes on the wrestling mats left me gasping for air. I wasn't prepared for the fact that wrestling works an entirely different set of muscles than running. Plus the constant contact with my opponent brought an end of me much more quickly. The next year I stuck with only soccer, but the comical experience has stayed with me a lifetime.

In today's reading we are about to see how God would bring Jacob to the end of himself. By using hardship as a discipline to his character, God allowed an extended season of basic training to unfold in Jacob's life. Finally the time came for the work to be completed, and guess what God used? A wrestling match! God would use this wrestling match to bring Jacob to the end of himself. Instead of receiving a prize at the end of the contest, Jacob was given a limp so the experience would last his lifetime.

Restlessness Leads to Wrestling

Before Jacob's life-changing wrestling match with God, he became restless. The twenty years of forced service and the ten wage cuts from Laban had taken their toll, and now we find Jacob devising a plan to separate from his uncle while enhancing his own bank account. Once again he practiced less-than-honorable ethics, which sent Laban into a hot pursuit for Jacob's life. Jacob got a head start by slipping out during the night, but Laban and his band of men quickly overcame him.

Trying to determine where he could go to find safety from the wrath of Laban, Jacob headed back to the place where he'd met God in a dream and eventually reached his homeland. Going this direction brought large risks to consider, but remaining with Laban just wasn't tolerable. The words of Henry Cloud describe Jacob in this situation. "We change our behavior when the pain of staying the same becomes greater than the pain of changing. Consequences give us the pain that motivates us to change."[1]

Almost identical to the scene twenty years earlier, Jacob fled for his life from his deceptive uncle but headed in the direction of a brother he assumed would extract revenge. Jacob was stuck between a rock and a hard place. No scheming or deceptive plan would work this time. In a moment of crisis Jacob did something that isn't recorded in Scripture since he received his dream twenty years earlier. He prayed!

This week's reading, along with our fourth winning principle, is about cultivating God dependence in our lives. I have learned firsthand that God often uses crises to bring us to our knees in prayer and nurture dependence on him.

Up to this point Jacob had solved all other crises through his abilities and talents of scheming and manipulation. But now he would have to rely on the mighty hand of God to do for him what he could never do for himself. This is a great definition of God dependence: trusting God to do only what he can do in and through our lives. Jacob was coming to the end of himself, and he needed a miracle from God—and boy did God show up in a unique way.

As Jacob and his family drew closer to the borders of his homeland, he sent his family ahead while he remained behind, probably to protect them from the wrath of Esau. Whether to protect his family or to have some time to himself, Jacob was alone, unprotected, and frightened.

It's interesting that Jacob's story began when he was alone at Bethel twenty years before, and he was alone once again before the long-awaited confrontation with his brother, Esau.

Let me give you another lesson I've learned over the years: God will use not only crises to birth dependence but also loneliness. Jacob was left alone in an ocean of a million stars above with only his thoughts. In essence God left Jacob alone with Jacob.

Certainly God in his foreknowledge knew he was going to touch Jacob's hip, so why did the wrestling match have to last so long?

Do you remember my wrestling story? I lasted five minutes while wrestling with an adolescent, underdeveloped, teenage boy. Jacob would endure hours of wrestling with the king of the universe. I can only imagine how exhausting and wearisome a match it was, but God wasn't concerned with time because he had lasting fruit in Jacob's life in mind. Said another way, transformation was taking place as Jacob struggled. The culmination of twenty years of "process" was at stake, and Jacob was on the verge of emerging as a new man.

I remember the story of a little girl who was observing a butterfly as it struggled to get out of its cocoon. She reached down to help it escape, but her dad immediately stopped her.

"Daddy, I was just trying to help," she explained. "It seems really hard and is taking forever!"

The father, having wisdom of what was really taking place, explained, "Honey, I know you are just trying to help, but the struggle is necessary. As the butterfly struggles to get free, blood is forced through its body into its wings, and that is how the butterfly is able to fly. That poor caterpillar waited long enough to become a butterfly. We don't want to ruin that for it, do we?"

To which the girl shouted, "No, Daddy. Never!" She then watched for hours until the butterfly finally emerged, its beautiful body able to fly away in its new environment. The truth is, struggle transforms us, because it brings us to the end of ourselves and forces the new man to emerge.

What came next for Jacob, however, seemed even stranger than the wrestling match itself. God touched his hip and gave him a limp for the rest of his life. This is a tough reality to wrap our minds around. Here Jacob was, at the end of a long season with Laban and about to meet Esau. He was on the verge of destiny, and God gave him a permanent disability. Why?

Let me answer the question by asking a few of my own. First, why does God allow certain adversities to come our way that may last a lifetime or at least feel like they are going to last forever? Second, we know we live in a fallen world where bad things happen to good people, but why does God allow some of those things to touch our lives? And third, why does God allow certain disabilities—whether they are physical, emotional, financial, or even relational—to remain in our lives even though we've prayed about them time and time again?

I guess my point is this: If we really think about it, we all limp in some way. God desires to use these shortcomings for the same purpose he had in mind for Jacob—to bring him to the end of himself. In fact, I no longer define a limp as a disability. I define it as an *in*ability. And it is through our inabilities that God brings forth his abilities in our lives. It is through our weakness that his strength is made perfect, and it is through our limited resources that God's unlimited resources are fully realized and embraced. The bottom line is that my "inability" produces a dependence within me for God's ability to take over in my life. God wants a consecration not only of our abilities but also our inabilities.

An invalid was told she could never escape from her prison of pain and weakness. "Oh, well," she replied quickly, "there's a lot of living to be found in your limitations, if you don't wear yourself out fighting them."

"Young lady," the doctor replied, "I wish I could have you preach to about a hundred of my patients a year."

The lady was Helen Keller, who said, "Face your deficiencies and acknowledge them, but don't let them master you."[2] Jacob's wings were about to come forth because of his affliction from God, and so will ours.

I love what happens next in our story; immediately after touching Jacob's hip, God said, "Let me go, for it is daybreak" (Gen. 32:26). Jacob reacted by saying, "I will not let you go unless you bless me." You have to admire Jacob's tenacity—after all, he relentlessly pursued Esau's blessing until he got it, and now he was pursuing God's blessing with the same fervency. He declared, "I will not let go until you bless me." This method is in stark contrast to the manipulating and deceitful measures he'd once applied to attain blessings. As it turns out, Jacob wasn't wrestling against God; he was wrestling for forgiveness, hope, and the real source of blessing.

Now Jacob was ready for the question of a lifetime. God asked him, "What is your name?" Of course, God knew his name, but Jacob needed to say it.

"Jacob," he answered. God asked this question to illustrate a principle we all must learn. To become who we are meant to be, we must admit who we really are. Let me add one more line to that: we must admit where we truly are if we are ever going to arrive at the place where we want to be. Jacob admitted, "I am Jacob…, the liar." Finally, his life was laid bare, desperate and dependent on God. And as a result of his honesty, God changed his name to Israel, which means "one who struggles with God and overcomes." It can also mean "prince with God." A new day was dawning for Jacob; his name was changed, and a new nature was born.

As dawn broke, Jacob left with a limp, a constant reminder of his need for God. A. W. Tozer once said, "Before God uses a man, he must wound him deeply."[3] This lasting "wound" would serve as a springboard for true humility to take root in Jacob's life. He was on the verge of destiny, but I have personally learned a vital truth about experiencing the fulfillment of God's plan for your life: God would rather that I limp into my destiny with humility than run into it with pride. Charles Spurgeon said, "Great hearts can only be made by great trouble."[4] This lasting limp for Jacob would serve as a trouble that would continue to mold a great heart and a great destiny through a spirit of humility and dependency on God.

Conclusion

So far, we have talked about God's developing dependence in our lives by giving us big dreams that demand we depend on a big God.

Jacob's ladder teaches us that the source of true blessing and dream fulfillment comes from the Lord. He also allows us to experience "basic training"—hardships that discipline our lives for a greater destiny. As we have seen today, he develops dependence through those things that cause us to "limp." Remember, our inability is the platform for God's ability to take over. If this is true, our limp isn't really a point of our weakness but of his strength. We will walk or limp into our destiny with humility, dependence, and the strength of the Lord.

These lessons are vital to fulfilling our hinge decision. The time will come when we will feel like giving up and throwing in the towel. We will stumble here and there and even experience moments of outright failure. And when that happens, we need to remember to shift our weight from our strength back to his. We must shift our focus from our failure to his success and from ourselves back to the Lord. We must practice his presence daily, remembering those internal acts of devotion we talked about on Day 21, and keep the Lord ever before us.

Finally, perhaps there's no other arena where our limp becomes more blatantly obvious to us than the arena of personal outreach. As you try to reach an unchurched person through this forty-day challenge, remember, the goal isn't to cover up the weaknesses in your life but to expose God's strength in the midst of them. It's important that the unchurched realize that becoming a Christian doesn't mean the absence of troubles but the presence of God in the midst of them. John 16:33 is a good verse for us to end on today as well as a good verse to share with our unchurched friend. "I have told you these things so that you may have peace. In this world you will have trouble. But take heart, I have overcome the world."

How about You?

1. Have you ever come to the "end of yourself "? What have you wrestled against that caused this to happen? Generally speaking, what is your response when this happens? Do you pause and pray? Do you become anxious and fearful? Do you try to work harder to make it happen?

2. How do you feel about A. W. Tozer's quote "Before God uses a man, he must wound him deeply"? Does this quote challenge your view of God at all, or do you see this statement as being consistent with Scripture? Have you personally experienced that God allows certain wounds to remain in our lives to ensure that we remain leaning on him?

3. We cannot underestimate the role of dependence when it comes to personal outreach. Sharing Christ with others isn't just about sharing a formula with them. It's about saying what God would have us say in any given circumstance. This is especially true when it comes to helping others through a time of crisis. Is there someone in your life who is dealing with a crisis and whom you can pray for? Can you share the truth with this person that God wants to be with him or her in the midst of what he or she is enduring?

Day 5: Jacob's Legacy

We ended yesterday with Jacob receiving a new name in Genesis 32. He limped away from his wrestling match as "Israel," which means "prince with God." What a contrast to his former name, "supplanter and deceiver." His journey had been a long one, his character had been dealt a heavy blow, and ultimately his destiny was shaped.

It would be easy to end our week with the image of Jacob as a new man limping into his destiny, but this is only partially true. For a time after his famous wrestling match, it was still uncertain whether we would see Jacob and his old way of doing things or Israel and his new way of doing things. This battle is similar to our own. We must choose daily to live according to the new man, not the old.

But still, Jacob's life and ultimately his legacy continue to teach some powerful lessons. Today I want to remind us of a few principles we have looked at this week and share a couple of others as we close out our study on dependence.

I Must Continually Grow into My New Name and Nature

After he received his new name, the very next chapter of Jacob's life began on a low note. Instead of acting like a "prince with God," he continued to act more like his old nature. Instead of following through on meeting with Esau, he lied to him again and traveled in the opposite direction. No doubt he did so out of fear…still. The two didn't meet again until they buried their father years later. Not only that, but Jacob couldn't quite get settled. He journeyed often and unnecessarily. Apparently, trusting the Lord was still very difficult for him. Acting as a prince with God was even harder.

Second Peter 1:1–10 is worth putting this book down and reading in full. Peter concluded verse 10 by saying, "Therefore, my brothers, be all the more eager to make your calling and election sure." He already reminded us that God's divine power had given us everything we need for life and godliness. Through God's glory and goodness, Peter continued, we have received incredible promises through which we can participate in the divine nature and escape the evil corruption in the world. But sandwiched between these powerful verses is verse 5, which reveals a key to living up to our new man. It starts off with, "For this very reason add to your faith," and then Peter listed many Christian attributes. In other words, Peter said, to walk in the new man, keep growing. Keep adding to your faith and refuse to stall and settle.

Romans 12:11 says, "Never be lacking in zeal, but keep your spiritual fervor, serving the Lord." In this day and time we must continue to move forward and grow if we are going to truly live a life marked by the new nature we have in Christ. Unlike the car we drive, there are only two gears for us to choose from when it comes to our faith: forward or reverse. "Neutral" really doesn't exist for believers. Those who try to "coast" always end up in reverse. We must be intentional about moving forward.

If You Should Drift, Go Back to Bethel

This reminds me of the time I took a group of students to the beach on a youth trip. I love the ocean, and I was always the kid (and adult) who loved to swim out as far as he could. However, I'll never forget swimming out in the ocean with this group of students on one of our afternoons together. It was perfect weather, and we were having fun throwing balls and enjoying the fellowship. Twenty minutes after swimming out as far as I deemed safe, I looked up to spot our beach towels and umbrellas for a point of reference. I should have known this would happen, but we had drifted at least one hundred yards from where we entered the water. We didn't intentionally do this. We were in the water, and the current just naturally moved us foot by foot as we were having fun. It was a bit scary to realize just how far you could drift in such a current, and it became more and more difficult to spot where we'd first entered the water.

In our society it is only natural that we will drift in our faith unless we intentionally swim in the direction of spiritual growth. Otherwise the stress of life, the temptations of our flesh, and the culture we live in will take us step by step away from our first love and away from who we truly are in Christ. And just as I looked up and tried to find where we'd entered the water at the beach that day, it will become harder and harder over time to find where we "went wrong." We will become victims of the so-called neutral gear—coasting further and further away from our true identity as Christians.

When this happens, we must do what Jacob (Israel) did in Genesis 35. He went back to Bethel. God spoke to him in 35:1 about this move. "Go up to Bethel and settle there, and build an altar there to God." God had him return to his "entry point," the place where God had spoken to him so powerfully years before, to recoup and restore his sense of new identity. Jacob named the place Bethel because the name means "house of God."[1] It represented the place where God began to deconstruct Jacob's old man and construct the new one. It represented the place where the first building blocks were laid in Jacob's journey.

I have often noticed that when a believer drifts in his or her faith, there is usually a failure with the fundamentals. At some point he or she stopped doing what produced growth and spiritual strides in his or her life. Usually, these things are what we would deem the basics of the faith such as spending time with God, going to church, and walking free from sinful entanglements. Throw in a dose of deception from the enemy, and it's not really hard to discern why it appears that a person has ended up far from a growing faith. If this has happened to you, return to Bethel. Return to the basics. Master the fundamentals again. Restore again the timeless building blocks for a growing faith.

Jacob wasted no time in doing this very thing. First, he cleaned house. He had his family rid themselves of all foreign gods. This is true spiritual leadership taking place in Jacob's life as the prince with God. It was his starting point, and it is ours.

We must rid ourselves of whatever has caused us to stumble if we are ever going to make genuine strides in our faith. Next, Jacob built an altar. An altar in the Old Testament represented a place of death, sacrifice, and commitment. Jacob recommitted himself and his family to the Lord. He then heard God remind him of his new name and of past promises. This is something we must do too. We must remind ourselves of who we are in Christ and recall the promises he has made.

Finally, Jacob settled in Bethel. He intentionally made sure the work of God had gotten into him deeply before hurrying to the next place. Again, we must do the same. Colossians 3:16 says, "Let the word of God dwell in you richly." We must allow the work of the Holy Spirit stir within us again, revive those internal acts of worship we spoke about on Day 22, and meditate on his work in our lives and on his word, including the word we are reading during our daily devotions.

The next phase of Jacob's life as Israel centers on his son, Joseph. Joseph was Jacob's next-to-last child, and guess what? He favored him! We will look at the life of Joseph next week, but for now, just know that Jacob continued the same type of favoritism his mother had showed him years and years earlier. This favor would cost him dearly, as his other sons devised a plot to rid Joseph from their lives, and Jacob would live under the impression for years that Joseph was dead.

As I look into this story, I'm convicted as a father to make sure that the weaknesses I have battled with don't become those of my sons. I know this sounds like a lot of pressure for a parent, but it's vital that we understand our role in passing on spiritual strengths to our children. I must simply conquer certain patterns and behaviors in my life so that my children won't have to fight the same battles in the future.

Israel's story ended after he and Joseph were reunited. How this happened is a great compliment to Jacob's determination to allow his new name to prevail in his final days. He and Joseph were estranged. Famine had taken over Israel's land. His other sons told him that Joseph was in Egypt with life-saving provision, and once again God appeared to Israel, telling him to go and trust him. Jacob did so without hesitation. He trusted the Lord, and the Bible specifically tells us that he did so as "Israel" (Gen. 46:1). After the reunion, Jacob made Joseph promise not to bury him in Egypt. Genesis 47:31 says that after Joseph makes this promise, "Israel worshiped as he leaned on the top of his staff."

This reminds me that what's important isn't how you start but how you finish. We started this week exploring Jacob's dependence and his "lean." We looked at how God dismantled Jacob's own strength, even by touching his hip and giving him a limp. We see Jacob at the end of his days, worshiping and leaning on the Lord. What a finish!

Conclusion

I want my kids to find me leaning on the Lord just as Joseph would observe in his father's final days. Not only that, but I want to end my life blessing my children the right way. Jacob did just that. Whereas early in life Jacob stole his father's blessing from Esau, he now blessed the legacy he was left behind. This truth causes me to admire Jacob, but it really causes me to wonder at God's ability to finish what he starts and to continuously extend his faithfulness and grace to me as I grow into the man he has called me to be. Furthermore, I'm reminded that my choice to depend on and trust the Lord makes this process easier.

If we aren't careful, we'll finish a week's worth of reading on the big story of Jacob and the big promises of God over his life, and we will wonder how life relates to ours. The answer is really quite simple. Though the promises and purposes of our lives might be different, the principle is the same. We, too, must learn to lean on the Lord. The man or woman we turn out to be hinges on this decision.

And speaking of hinges, we too will leave our own legacy in part by fulfilling commitments we are making today, such as our hinge decisions. Remember, you've been challenged not just to make a decision but to make one life-changing decision. Certainly, if you follow through on this decision and it changes your life, it has the potential to change the outcome of the legacy you leave. It can affect your children, the next generation, and the bigger picture of your family line. I'm not sure about you, but I'm now convinced through the life of Jacob that a godly family line begins with the family's choice of which way to lean. May we be found like Israel—leaning on his staff and worshiping the Lord.

How about You?

1. What difficulties do you face when it comes to growing into your new name? What things from the past can easily trip you up? Have any of these things jeopardized the fulfillment of your hinge decision?

2. We talked about Jacob returning to Bethel and refusing to drift. What can you do to avoid drifting spiritually in your life? Remember, there is no neutral ground! What intentional things must you do to keep your spiritual fervor (Heb. 12:11)?

3. Our lives are books our children read as they grow up. Certainly, there are chapters we are proud of and others we aren't. However, are you really determined that what your children conclude about your life is defined as a life that leaned on and trusted the Lord? Are they currently drawing that conclusion based on this chapter of your life?

CHAPTER 5:

WEEK 5—MY DREAM

Day 1: Here Comes That Dreamer!

Welcome to Week 5 of *A Life That Wins*. This week we are looking into the life of Joseph. His story best exemplifies the fifth quality of a winning life: the willingness to dream. Joseph's dream is found in Genesis 37, and there he sees his entire family bowing down to him. What most people don't realize is that Joseph was only seventeen years old at the time. Telling others about his dream was somewhat expected considering his excitement about God speaking to him, his immaturity, and his touch of pride. What Joseph didn't expect was the pushback from every member of his family, including his father.

Because everyone clearly understood that Joseph was his father's favorite, his brothers viewed this dream as one more example of boasting about his favored position. It didn't sit well with his brothers. The story resumes sometime later when his brothers took their herd of sheep to better pastures some distance away. As was the pattern for Old Testament farming communities, someone had to take meals to the men out in the fields. This job normally fell to the younger members of the family, so as expected Joseph was given the task of delivery boy. From a distance his brothers saw him coming, and in Genesis 37:19, they gritted their teeth, saying, "Here comes that dreamer!"

Joseph's brothers didn't compliment him by any means, but their statement strikes a chord within me. The truth is, I'm a dreamer, and I want to be known as such. Granted, I don't want to be known as an arrogant dreamer, but I do want to be known as someone who is willing to believe God for the impossible, to take God-sized risks when they are his will, and simply to never be afraid to "go for it" when it comes to his plans for my life.

After all, isn't this dreamer's spirit cultivated within us at a young age? How many times have I already asked my kids, "What is your dream?" And how many times were we asked in grade school, "What do you want to be when you grow up?" I'm reminded of a story I once heard about the power of dreaming.

It started like so many evenings: Mom and Dad at home and Jimmy playing after dinner. Mom and Dad were absorbed with jobs and didn't notice the time. It was a full moon, and some of the light seeped through the windows. Then Mom glanced at the clock.

"Jimmy, it's time to go to bed. Go up now, and I'll come and settle you later."

Unlike usual, Jimmy went straight upstairs to his room. An hour or so later his mother came up to check on whether all was well. To her astonishment she found that her son was staring out his window at the moonlit scenery.

"What are you doing, Jimmy?"

"I'm looking at the moon, Mommy."

"Well, it's time to go to bed now."

As the reluctant boy settled down, he said, "Mommy, you know, one day I'm going to walk on the moon."

Who could have known that the boy in whom the dream was planted that night would later in life survive a near-fatal motorbike crash, breaking almost every bone in his body? And how could one have known that thirty-two years later he would bring to fruition this dream of the moon when James Irwin stepped on the moon's surface, only one of twelve human beings to have done so?[1]

When we were young, the sky was the limit, but as we grow older, reality or—better said—life sets in. Life becomes full of complicated decisions, and the world of endless possibilities becomes the world of endless responsibilities. We're forced to answer the unwelcome wake-up call where the message on the other end of the line is, "It's time to grow up!" We can easily lose grip on our dream and end up with a job that pays the bills and not necessarily a purpose that drives us every day.

As one who travels and speaks to all age groups across the nation, I would say the above scenario describes many young adults today. The danger is that many sorely lack direction and can remain adrift in life well into their late twenties and early thirties. For this reason I teach a conference called EQUIP (http://www.mikeholtonline.com/EQUIP). Through the conference I outline the reasons this problem has become a reality in America's culture, and I offer suggestions for parents about how to guide young people through this life-defining season.

The truth is, our kids have become a product of their culture and the parenting paradigms of this day and time. If we aren't intentional in a few key areas, a younger generation can wander aimlessly for years with no sense of real purpose or destiny.

But I have good news! God has dreams and visions for our lives regardless of our current age and employment status. Whether we're older adults working a job we aren't really passionate about or young people who are currently seeking direction, God has a dream for our lives. Typically God gives us dreams by

- reviving old dreams within us that have gone dormant for some reason;
- giving us new dreams to strive for; and
- infusing a sense of purpose within us for what we are currently doing in life. God may not have a whole new dream for us. He might just want to give us a dream for what we are already doing.

Whatever category you fall into, God wants us dreaming again. Today's reading is a reminder of three things God uses to reveal these dreams for our lives.

God Uses Prayer to Help Me Discern My Purpose

First Corinthians 2:9–10 says, "No eye has seen, no ear has heard, no mind has conceived what God has planned for those that love him. But he reveals it by his Spirit." This verse tells us two things: First, God has incredible things planned for my life. Second, he reveals it by his Spirit. As we pray, stay connected, and touch his heart, God reveals his plan for us one step at a time.

I have personally learned to acknowledge restraint and the release of the Holy Spirit in my life. Three years ago, I dreamed about Reach the City, the campaign this book is connected to for the local church. We experimented with the concepts, methods, and approach to personal outreach that is the core of Reach the City...with huge success.

However, the following weekend I was in a hotel room in Louisville, Kentucky, praying over Reach the City and excited about all that would lie ahead, and I sensed the restraint of the Holy Spirit in regard to taking any other action on this dream. It confused me greatly, to be honest with you. Here I was, having just "proved" this campaign could work, and now God was putting me on pause.

Three years later I felt a release in launching Reach the City. Weeks later I received a text message from a businessman who was willing to finance the development of key ingredients for Reach the City. You could describe this series of events as God's putting me on pause for three years, but the truth is, it would have taken me ten years to raise the amount of funds necessary to launch this ministry. God knew best—imagine that!

Through prayer we sense the release and restraint of the Holy Spirit, and our steps become ordered and directed as we strive to fulfill our dreams.

God Uses His Principles to Help Me Discover My Purpose

In his book *Visioneering*, Andy Stanley describes vision as "a clear mental picture of something that could be fueled by the conviction that it ought to be."[2] You need to read that definition again...It is powerful! A dream or vision isn't just a picture of something that *could* be; it's a picture fueled by the conviction that it *ought* to be. We dream about many things that could be, but often our God-given dreams are birthed not only from something that *could* happen but from something that *should* happen. As we are convinced that the dreams in our hearts must be fulfilled, there is a conviction that turns the dream into a cause.

One way to discern our dream is to ask ourselves, "What am I really convicted about?" When my wife was growing up, God placed a huge burden on her heart for families in ministry. She'd seen many ministry families struggle greatly as a result of what life in ministry involved. From this, a picture was formed in her spirit of what a healthy ministry family could look like. Our family isn't perfect by any means, but it's healthy in large part because of the convictions of my wife.

How about you? Is there anything in your life you're convinced could be and, more importantly, should be? Is there anything you've had a burden about for quite sometime and perhaps you haven't moved on yet? This burden could be the very building block for an unfulfilled dream in your life.

John W. Gardner, founding chairman of Common Cause, said it's a rare and high privilege to help people understand the difference they can make—not only in their own lives but also in the lives of others—simply by giving of themselves.

Gardner tells of a cheerful old man who asked the same question of just about every new acquaintance he fell into conversation with. "What have you done that you believe in and are proud of ?"

He never asked conventional questions such as, "What do you do for a living?" It was always, "What have you done that you believe in and are proud of ?"

It was an unsettling question for people who had built their self-esteem on their wealth, their family name, or their exalted job title.

Not that the old man was a fierce interrogator. He was delighted when a woman answered, "I'm doing a good job raising three children" and when a cabinetmaker said, "I believe in good workmanship and practice it" and when a woman said, "I started a bookstore, and it's the best bookstore for miles around."

"I don't really care how they answer," the old man said. "I just want to put the thought into their minds.

"They should live their lives in such a way that they can have a good answer. Not a good answer for me, but for themselves. That's what's important."[3]

God Uses My Passions to Help Me Discover My Purpose

This is also a simple but often overlooked principle. We tend to believe that God's dream for our lives, once discovered, is going to make us miserable. It's what I call "the jungle dream." You know, if you really love Jesus, then he is going to call you to the jungle in some remote part of the world. After all, we think, those are the only kinds of dreams God gives, and even though they have nothing to do with our personality and passions, we'd better obey. To be miserable is to be spiritual, and if my dream isn't as big as the jungle, I'm just not Christian enough.

I'm being slightly sarcastic, of course. I have friends who actually are jungle missionaries. It's been a tough road, but they know they are exactly where they are supposed to be. But the tendency is to compare my dream to theirs and say that if my dream isn't that "big," then I'm not good enough, or somehow I've missed God. This is a huge misconception about dreaming. In fact, I would venture to say that God wants to use some of the very passions he has placed within us to fulfill the overall purpose for our lives.

If I love kids, then there's probably a dream to uncover. Sure, the dream could mean going overseas as a children's missionary; it could also mean helping out in your children's church. You might love to fish. I'm not sure if there are missionary fishermen, but you could certainly start an interest-based small group where you help disciple men or introduce men to Jesus who might not darken the door of a local church. Charles Kingsley said, "We act as though comfort and luxury were the chief requirements of life, when all that we need to make us really happy is something to be enthusiastic about."[4]

Ask yourself, "What do I love to do, and how could God take this passion to a greater level of purpose in and through my life?" Once again, there are plenty of things that catch our eye. These are the things that could be. The question is, what captures your heart? That is the thing that *ought* to be. Answer that question, and you might be on to something.

God Uses My Past to Help Me Discover My Purpose

Some of the biggest purposes come from the greatest points of pain in our lives. As I said about the life of Leah in Week 3, God wants to use our past to help powerfully shape the future of somebody else. Your greatest struggle could become your greatest strength. Your greatest problem could be the greatest platform you have for God-given purpose to explode in your life. This is why so many former drug addicts are now sponsors for people trying to come off drugs. This is why so many men who didn't have a good positive male role model while growing up are now some of the greatest Little League coaches. And this is why so many women who were abused are now the greatest source of encouragement to teenage girls who need life-changing love. Ask yourself, "Is there anything that I have walked through in my past that could offer a sense of purpose in my present?"

Consider the late Charles Colson, who went to jail for his role as Richard Nixon's aide in the Watergate scandal. As a result of his experience as a convicted felon, Colson founded Prison Fellowship, now the world's largest Christian outreach to prisoners and their families. Prison Fellowship has more than fifty thousand volunteers working in hundreds of prisons in eighty-eight countries around the world. A ministry that has blessed millions of people got started because Charles Colson committed a crime.[5]

Conclusion

Joseph had a dream—and a big one at that. His brothers looked at him from a distance, mocking him in anger as he drew closer and closer. What would follow was a seventeen-year journey Joseph would endure before his dream came true. It involved a pit, a prison, a palace, and ultimately a fulfilled promise—but not until both the dream and the dreamer matured. In the following days we will look closely at the maturity process of every dream.

For now, as we close out today, my prayer is that you will be encouraged to dream again. Allow God to blow dust off old dreams if that's necessary. Or allow God to birth something new in you—or again maybe to instill within you fresh vision and purpose for what you are currently doing right now. As all this relates to your hinge decision, the question is, what dream is your decision advancing? You made a decision probably because there was already a conviction that something ought to change and look differently in your life. Let me ask you this: now that we are five weeks into this journey together, can you tell a difference in your life as you've fulfilled your one life-changing decision? Is the vision for what could be just as real in your life today, Day 29, as it was on Day 1? What's the vision behind your change? What's the "why" behind what you are trying to change with God's help? Continue to answer these questions, and you will continue to strive to ensure that your one life-changing decision remains permanent.

How about You?

1. Take a few minutes and answer the questions posed in today's reading:

    - Is there any area of your life where you feel the restraint or release of the Holy Spirit? Is there an area of your life where God is saying, "Speed up," but you are slowing down? Or any area where he is saying, "Slow down," but you are trying to speed up?

- What in life convicts you? What need do you see in everyday life and are compelled to meet?

- What captures your heart, not just your eye? What is something you are really passionate about that could become a purpose in your life?

- What from your past could become a point of purpose in your life?

2. For those of you engaged in the Reach the City campaign, yesterday could have served as a "friend day" for your church. If you had an unchurched friend attend church with you yesterday, what are you doing to follow up with him or her? Remember to use our website for practical ideas to follow up with guests to your church, and remember to attend the last two weeks of your challenge group (http://www.reachthecity.com/effectivefollowup).

Day 2: Time, Sand, and Water

I'm noise sensitive. There, I admit it. Gum popping, pencil tapping, knuckle cracking, and babies crying can get on my nerves. At least I'm honest about it. That's why I remember the day I woke up to this grinding, whining, click-clacking sound in my garage. "Did I leave a tool on? What in the world?" I thought. I asked my oldest son, Jake, if I was hearing things.

He said, "No, Dad. I'm making precious rubies in the garage!"

"Do what?" I asked.

"Yeah, I finally got the rock tumbler you gave me for Christmas working!" He was so excited, but I wasn't.

"Your what?"

"My rock tumbler, Daddy!"

I didn't even remember my wife getting him something called a rock tumbler. It was something I'd never heard of until it woke me up that morning.

I walked into the garage and found the source of noise. Sure enough, it was a barrel about the size of a small football spinning round and round like a rotisserie chicken. The machine in that gadget was working overtime.

"What in the world does this do, Jake?"

He explained the process. A rock tumbler is a kit for refining a rock, maybe into a gemstone. You can Google these online and see them in massive form doing what this little one was supposedly doing. Jake, my seven-year-old, then proceeded to give me a science lesson.

"Dad, the rock tumbler comes with this rock. It's big and rugged, but you put it in this container and turn it on, and it eventually becomes a shiny jewel." I had a feeling this process was going to take some time.

"What exactly does it take for this rock to become a ruby, Jake?"

"Not much, Dad. Just a lot of time, sand, and water," he said.

And he wasn't kidding! This stupid rock tumbler became my alarm clock for about three months. Periodically, Jake would change the water and add sand, which was empowering the transformation to take place.

I have to admit that the little jewels this thing produced when it was all over were pretty cool. But boy, did it ever take time, sand, and a little water.

I've noticed that dreams also require these three components. They take time and aren't fulfilled overnight. They also take sand. Sand is the thing that refines our dream and us. And water is the touch of promise God gives us along the way to just keep us going.

Time

Nobody likes it when God seems to take his time. For Joseph, seventeen years passed before his dream was fulfilled. And they were seventeen years apart from his family in an unknown land—Egypt of all places. Maybe you've heard the Crock-Pot-versus-microwave example. God is a Crock-Pot, not a microwave. There are promises from God that are "slow cooked," but in the end they are well worth it when we finally sink our teeth into them and experience them. Furthermore, we cannot treat God or our dreams like a bag of popcorn in a microwave. They simply don't cook in two and a half minutes, and they don't pop out for a quick and ready-to-eat snack. Dreams take time. Most of us know that.

However, it's one thing to see your dream in God's Crock-Pot, and it's another to see yourself in it. The truth is, the two are inseparable. Our dreams take time to mature because *we* take time to mature and bear much fruit in our lives.

When I was growing up one of my favorite meals was when my father smoked chicken. The process would take six hours, and occasionally he would open the little door on the side of the smoker and add more vegetables or "secret sauce" to give the meat that little extra flavor. I can still taste my dad's chicken to this day because the process was worth it, and that little extra seasoning made all the difference in the world. The same is true for us. I've realized that God seasons us most when he seems to be taking his time. As I travel some of my favorite pastors to preach for are those who are closest to retirement. There is something that inspires me to be with seasoned saints who have matured deeply over time.

This is exactly what would have transpired over time with Joseph. As a seventeen-year-old, Joseph was overzealous and probably a little full of himself to prematurely share his dream of being front and center of it all. But at the end of the seventeen years, we find a Joseph interpreting the dreams of others and advising Pharaoh on how to govern in the midst of a nationwide famine. From the life of Joseph, we learn that dreaming is one thing, but having the willingness and wisdom to execute a dream is something else. The latter takes time to cultivate but is absolutely essential to seeing our dreams become reality.

Sand

But then there is the sand. Remember, the sand is the substance in the rock tumbler that polishes and transforms a rock into, as my son said, "a precious jewel." The truth is, without the sand, there would be no transformation in that rock tumbler. Without sand in our lives, there is no transformation either. Think about the sand in Joseph's journey. Consider the following:

- **The pit**—His brothers mocked him and threw him in a cistern. Nobody believed in his dream. Have you ever felt this way? Or, what's worse, have you stepped out in faith in the past and fallen flat on your face? Now, perhaps you don't even believe in your own dreams. And then there is always the devil who will do all he can to instill doubt into our hearts. If we aren't careful, he will talk us out of what God is trying to talk us into.
- **The prison**—Tomorrow we will look in a little more depth at the prison where Joseph spent three years. For now the punch line is that Joseph spent time in prison, not for something he did wrong, but for something he did right. He ended up in

prison because of his integrity and character. In fact, the last three years of his seventeen years in Egypt could have been the hardest for Joseph. I've realized that just before dreams become reality, the last phase of the maturing process can be the hardest. The Lord zeros in on issues of the heart, bringing freedom to the areas of our lives that could one day jeopardize our dream. Natural circumstances can become tougher, as we must navigate difficult issues such as making time for our dream or even financing it. Those closest to us might challenge us the most as we move closer to stepping into our dream. They aren't necessarily being negative, but they will issue good, honest questions that must be answered. The list goes on and on, but it's important to realize that sometimes we end up wrestling through certain battles because of what we've done right, not what we've done wrong. Call them growing pains if you wish, but they can be very trying and very refining.

- **The palace**—This seems like a hard one to include under the "sand" category, but bear with me. When Joseph came out of the prison, he was promoted from serving the warden to serving the entire nation. Talk about an increase in responsibilities. I've experienced in my own life that "arriving" at a new level doesn't relieve me of sand; it introduces me to an entirely new beach. Think about the young lady who has always dreamed of having children. The first baby is born, and it's a joy. But there are sleepless nights, eating schedules, and an entire life change to deal with. Think about the dad who has always dreamed of coaching his son's football team. It's a dream come true for sure, but it can feel like a nightmare when every other dad thinks he can do a better job than you and when you have that one mother who is always questioning why little Johnny isn't the quarterback. Think about the job promotion. The pay increase is great, but now you must contend with leading a larger team, and if your department isn't growing, it's your tail on the line. You get the point. Making it to the palace—however that is

> defined for you—can bring with it a dump truck full of fresh sand God will use to continue his process of refining your life. Take heart when this happens. If God were faithful to get you there, he will be faithful to grow you there.

Sand can be a great irritant. Get a little in your shoe, and you can take the shoe off and shake it out. Get a little of it in your life, and you are forced into a place where the only choice you can really make is to submit to the refinement process. After all, God is turning a rock into a ruby and a stone into a precious jewel.

Water

But thank God for water! Every morning, my son would check the tumbler and make sure the water level was where it needed to be for the process of transformation to continue. Scripture says in Lamentations 3:22, "His mercies are new every morning." Thank God for his mercy, which waters our souls. Not only that, but Jesus called himself the "living water." Time in his presence waters our souls. In John 7:38, Jesus said, "Whoever believes in me, as Scripture has said, rivers of living water will flow from within them." My very faith in him waters my soul. When I'm weary, I can recall his character, and confidence begins to flow again through my veins. When I pause and remember his promises, my faith level is elevated once again, and my soul is watered. His presence and his promises never leave me spiritually dehydrated.

Other than with his presence and his promises, what else do we water our dreams with? For me, time with my accountability partner, Thomas, waters my soul. He too is an entrepreneur, and we have faced some similar struggles in making our dreams reality. Time with him waters my soul.

Reading leadership material and listening to podcasts are also a source of refreshment for me. I not only glean valuable insight, but the teachings of like-minded leaders spur me on and encourage me to keep dreaming. Some of my most productive thinking, writing, and speaking happen on the heels of listening to or reading someone who waters my soul. Lastly, taking a day off, enjoying a favorite hobby, and getting alone by myself for a couple of hours do a lot of good in keeping my dreams well watered. What waters your dream? What waters your soul? As my son taught me about the rock tumbler, you have to keep an eye on the water level daily.

Conclusion

Time, sand, and water are the components not only of a rock tumbler but also of the ingredients of a wilderness season in your life. But take heart; God led the children of Israel through a desert before they could possess the promised land. Study the lives of those who made it into the hall of faith in Hebrews 11, and you will soon discover deep seasons of wilderness and desert these men and women endured.

Look at the life of Paul, and you'll see a man who disappeared for three years after his amazing Damascus road conversion. Many theologians believe this period was an initial desert season God used to prepare a great destiny.

Finally, turn in your Bible to Luke 4, and you'll find Jesus, driven into the desert by the Spirit of God for forty days to be tempted by the devil. Read through this story closely, and you'll discover verse 14: "And Jesus returned in the power of the Spirit." He was driven into the desert, only to come out in the power of the Spirit. The purpose of this process for Jesus is the same for us as we go round and round in the rock tumbler. We emerge in God's power and with his wisdom to execute the dreams he has placed in our hearts.

Chances are, if you've truly determined to follow through on your hinge decision, you might have experienced some sand in the tumbler you weren't expecting. Perhaps things got harder before they got easier. Perhaps you've executed some life change with God's help, but now the new measure of maturity has brought with it an entirely new bag of sand to contend with. Stay in the tumbler and let God finish his work. Check the water level daily and water your dreams with the right hoses. Don't become impatient with the time it takes for God to season you. The process will be worth it.

How about You?

1. Time: How long have you been dreaming certain dreams?

2. Sand: What is the sand in your tumbler God is using to refine you and your dream?

3. Water: What do you water your dream with? How do you water your soul?

Day 3: When God Backs Up, Keep Swimming

Can you endure just one more kid story? A great privilege of parenthood is teaching your kids how to swim. One of my boys was easy to teach; he took to the water like a fish. My other son, in keeping with how he does most things in life, wouldn't touch the deep end until he was good and ready. During a friend's birthday party, of his own accord he jumped into the deep end and swam as though he was born for the water.

With my daughter the experience was a different story altogether. First, everything for her is a fashion show. Second, she is our last child, our only girl, spoiled sweet, very methodical, and orderly in everything she does. Her swimming lessons took on her personality when she came out of her room dressed in a sparkly swimsuit with matching Crocs, earplugs, and goggles. I took her to the neighborhood pool, convinced that today would be the day she would swim in deep waters.

Standing at the edge of the steps, she said, "Daddy, stay right there." I nodded, and she jumped from the first step into my arms. To say the least, she was so proud of herself (I can only imagine where she gets that from). I lovingly informed her that she had only jumped and hadn't actually swum; I placed her back on the steps. "Daddy, don't back up."

I just smiled. Notice, I didn't agree with her; I just smiled. She jumped in and started dog-paddling toward me—and guess what I did? Yep. I backed up and up.

You could see the look of shock on her face as she was trying to burn a hole into my soul with her eyes while spitting water at the same time. You can probably imagine what she was thinking. "How could you, Daddy?" I stopped when the water reached a height of five feet. She tackled my head and nearly dunked me. I immediately pulled her close, as she was about to let me have it. Before she was able to gather enough breath to let loose on her dad, she looked behind her and realized how far she'd actually swum.

"Did I do that?" she exclaimed in shock. With pride and amazement she embraced me, realizing I had been a good father and not an evil one when I decided to back up and make her swim beyond what she thought was possible. I knew the endurance was in her, and the entire process pulled out of her what was already there.

Have you ever felt like God was backing up and teaching you to swim in deeper waters? You knew he was there, but he seemed just out of reach. Be encouraged. God isn't being evil. He's actually being good and teaching you to pursue him and your dreams with a relentless pursuit.

The process pulls the potential out of you just like it did for Joseph. After his brothers threw him into a pit, he endured a grueling journey to Egypt, shackled as a slave. He was then sold to the Egyptian named Potiphar, whose wife falsely accused him of attempted rape. He ended up in prison for three years, was forgotten by a cellmate for whom he helped achieve freedom, and was finally remembered after a season that could have easily caused him to quit on life and on God. But he didn't. He continued to swim and as a result came out of the pit with the wisdom to execute a dream that would cause the fulfillment of his own dreams. Throughout Joseph's story we see an individual of incredible commitment to the dream God had given him. There are three key decisions Joseph made that kept his dream alive.

Joseph Didn't Allow What Was Lost in One Season to Keep Him from Seizing What Would Be Gained in the Next

While in Potiphar's house, Joseph attained a position where others were subject to him, even though he was a slave himself. I wonder how many times Joseph thought, This must be it! God is fulfilling my dream from when I was just seventeen! But then, because of his integrity, he lost his position, and what appeared to be the fulfillment of his dream escaped like the wind.

Have you ever felt "so close yet so far away"? I'm sure Joseph did, and though he was thrown into the stench and violence of prison, Scripture doesn't describe him as being in despair or discouraged. In fact, he went right back to work, serving the prison warden and making the most of his circumstances, even though his dream seemed like an even greater distance from any possibility of becoming a reality. As a result his persistence positioned him to be the interpreter of his cell mate's dream, and the cell mate, who was the royal cupbearer, would then be the messenger to Pharaoh of the interpreting skills of Joseph. Persistence pays off!

Many dreamers find themselves in this place, feeling imprisoned and immobilized by fear or failure throughout the dreaming process. Some step out and fall flat on their faces and must make a decision to get back up and start over. Others attain a certain level of success, but the learning curve required to take the dream from one level to the next can be so overwhelming that it causes paralysis. And for some, their dream is something they flirt with in their thoughts but feel as though fulfillment is a marathon away. Whatever the case, you cannot let one season of life, whether defined by fear or failure, keep you from making the most of the next opportunity God brings to you.

Michael Jordan experienced this reality, not just with every season of his career, but with every shot he took. He is widely thought of as the best player in NBA history, but he's quoted as saying, "I've missed more than nine thousand shots in my career. I've lost almost three hundred games. Twenty-six times I've been trusted to take the game winning shot and missed. I've failed over and over and over again in my life. That is why I succeed."[1] Just because we miss one shot doesn't mean we don't take the next. And just because we "miss it" in one season doesn't mean we can't seize the moment in the next season. Keep being faithful. Keep shooting. Keep swimming!

Even Though He Was in an Ungodly Atmosphere, Joseph Maintained a Godly Attitude

Potiphar's wife was a very promiscuous woman who made sexual advances toward Joseph day after day. The Scripture tells us she tried to seduce him, but each time he refused her advances by saying, "How can

I do such a wicked thing and sin against my God?" He demonstrated tremendous character, but it wasn't rewarded—his character landed him in prison. Please take note of this once again. Joseph ended up in prison, not for what he did wrong, but for what he did right.

We sometimes end up in a "prison" type of experience, not because of what we've done wrong, but because of what we've done right. Joseph ended up in a lonely place, stripped once again of his coat that represented Potiphar's favor. Remember, this was the second time Joseph's coat was stripped from him, and he was left in dire circumstances. But Joseph made a series of critical decisions:

- Others could take his cloak but not his character. He chose to please God, even when his choice displeased others.
- Not only that, but he didn't lose his communion with God. While he was in prison, he looked to the Lord for help and restoration.
- Finally, he lost his cloak but not his compassion. He didn't allow his circumstances to produce a hardened heart. In fact, when two of Pharaoh's officials ended up in prison, Joseph was found showing concern for one of them, whose face appeared saddened. Joseph took interest in others, even though others lost interest in him. Amazingly, this gesture of compassion was the very thing that would grant him pardon, position, fulfillment, and much, much more.

A commitment to his calling, a communion with God in the midst of conflict, and a heart of compassion all comprised Joseph's character. The truth is, character is a rare commodity in today's world. Choosing to work hard on the job is difficult, even though everyone else is taking advantage of the system. Studying hard for a test is difficult when you could easily cheat. Refusing to look at pornography can be difficult, even though nobody would ever know. Demonstrating character is tough and can leave us feeling lonely in the midst of a culture where compromise is a cancer plaguing the workplace, schools, and even the home.

However, choosing to avoid immorality like Joseph did is one thing, but what about choosing character in the details of daily life? These are the hardest areas in which to maintain godly character, because there are so many issues we must daily contend with. And like Joseph, we contend with them, not because of anything we've done wrong, but just because we're living life and trying to live right.

For example, strong-willed children are difficult for any parent, and the parent must learn to navigate the best way to raise his or her child on a daily basis. Working on your marriage and growing through marital conflict instead of throwing in the towel are daily and often very taxing and heavy decisions. Expressing patience to that annoying coworker and choosing to serve a demanding boss don't necessarily mean we've chosen the wrong job. It can be the right job but with some hard factors to endure. These are a small sampling of the issues we all face as they relate to our desire to truly live with character and godliness.

This reminds me of an old story I recently read about a young Chinese wife trying to contend with her new mother-in-law. A long time ago, a newly married girl named Li-li couldn't get along with her mother-in-law, who lived with the newlyweds. Their personalities and habits clashed. They never stopped arguing and fighting., and traditionally Li-li had to bow to her mother-in-law and obey her every wish.

Finally, Li-li couldn't stand her mother-in-law's bad temper and dictatorship any longer. Li-Li went to see a family friend, Mr. Huang, who sold her herbs, told him the situation, and asked for some poison to slip into her mother-in-law's meals. She even agreed to do whatever Mr. Huang told her. Mr. Huang then gave her a package of herbs and told Li-li, "To eliminate suspicion, I have given you a number of herbs to slowly build up poison in her body. Every other day prepare some pork or chicken and put a little of these herbs in her serving. Also, act very friendly toward her so that nobody suspects you when she dies. Don't argue with her, obey her every wish, and treat her like a queen."

Li-li began serving the specially prepared food to her mother-in-law. She controlled her temper, obeyed her mother-in-law, and treated her like her own mother. For the next six months, Li-li was almost never upset or rarely had an argument with her kinder and friendlier mother-in-law. They were like mother and daughter.

In horror Li-li went to Mr. Huang and pleaded tearfully, "Mr. Huang, please help me to keep the poison from killing my own mother-in- law! She's changed into such a nice woman, and I love her like my own mother. I don't want her to die."

Mr. Huang comforted her. "Li-li, I never gave you any poison. I gave you vitamins to improve her health. The only poison was in your mind and your attitude."[2]

Doing the right thing in a hard situation is difficult, but in the end we must trust that our character will be rewarded. It most certainly was for Joseph.

Though Joseph Was Forgotten, He Chose to Forgive

The two individuals I just spoke about, the men who ended up in prison with Joseph, were Pharaoh's cupbearer and baker. Obviously they upset Pharaoh, and he had them tossed into prison while they awaited trial. In the meantime both had troubling dreams, and Joseph interpreted them correctly. Just as Joseph had interpreted in the dream, the baker was executed, and the cupbearer was restored to his position. However, after Joseph interpreted their dreams, he specifically asked the cupbearer to remember him if by chance he ever had the opportunity to tell Pharaoh that Joseph was the one who'd interpreted the dreams correctly. But the cupbearer completely forgot about him. His brothers, Potiphar's wife, and the cupbearer misunderstood and mistreated him. He could have easily become bitter, sulking in the feeling of being forgotten, but instead he extended grace and forgiveness throughout his journey.

One thing that helped Joseph forgive those who had mistreated him was the big-picture perspective he must have maintained throughout his journey. This is revealed in Genesis 50:20 when he looked at his brothers and said, "You intended to harm me, but God intended it for the good, for the saving of many lives."

I don't believe his response is "hindsight is twenty-twenty" at play. The work ethic and character Joseph demonstrated throughout the seventeen-year process were indicators that he kept his dream in front of him and trusted God to use *all* things, including betrayal and false imprisonment, for his good. Can you see how Joseph was convinced that nothing and no one could stop the fulfillment of his dream if he would remain faithful to the Lord? This sure makes forgiving others easier when we are relying on God's faithfulness toward us and not man's faithfulness to fulfill our lives and dreams.

In 1605 Squanto, a Native American from the village of Patuxet and a member of the Pokanokit Wampanoag nation, traveled to England with an explorer named John Weymouth. Squanto experienced high adventure and learned some English.

But on his return to America, the tide turned against Squanto. An English ship captain captured him from Massachusetts and took him, along with other Indians, and sold them into slavery in Málaga, Spain.

There a Spanish monk bought Squanto, treated him well, freed him from slavery, and taught him the Christian faith. Squanto eventually made his way to England, where he improved his English, and worked in the stables of a man named John Slaney. Slaney sympathized with Squanto's desire to return home and promised to put the Indian on the first vessel bound for America.

It wasn't until 1618—ten years after Squanto was first kidnapped—that he was on a ship and returning to America as a free man.

There he learned about the second blow the English had delivered. His tribe had died from an epidemic, probably of smallpox brought by the earlier colonists. He and another Indian, Samoset, went to live with the neighboring tribe of the Wampanoag near present-day Plymouth, Massachusetts. There he was introduced to the new Pilgrim settlers. And there Squanto became a picture of forgiveness. Even though the English had captured him and deprived him of family and friends because of their disease, he still chose to help the 47 of 102 Pilgrims who had barely survived their first, harsh winter. He helped them build warm houses and taught them when to plant their corn crop and how it should be planted. Without his help there wouldn't have been twenty acres of corn produced that year. Squanto also advised the Pilgrims in their relationships with the Indians. He helped them make friends, acted as interpreter, guided them on trading expeditions, and gave advice on bargaining with the natives. The Pilgrims wouldn't have made it through the year without the wisdom and guidance of Squanto.[3]

Conclusion

When my little girl came out of the water on the day I backed up and made her swim into the deep end, I looked at her and said, "I knew you could do it!" My confidence in the things I had been teaching her was the very reason I knew she could swim in deeper waters. The same is true with God and his relationship toward us. He is confident that the work he is doing in our lives will serve as a mighty platform for us to fulfill his will. We must simply continue to swim by taking hold of the lessons he is teaching us, keeping our character at all costs, and refusing to allow our hearts to become hardened toward others or God.

As we seek to fulfill our one hinge decision and reach others who don't know Christ, we must remain persistent and confident that he who began a good work in us is faithful to complete it (Phil. 1:6). And as you start swimming in deeper waters, seeing your dreams become reality, and reaching others along the way, God will surely look to you and say, "I knew you could do it!"

How about You?

1. Have you ever felt like you've been in a season where either God or your dreams are backing up on you, just out of reach? What did you learn from this season?

2. What character traits do you need to uphold with persistent determination as you continue to strive for your dream? What are some character traits that are strong and some that are weak in your life?

3. Do you easily forgive others? Is there someone you need to start extending more grace to at this time of your life? How does walking in grace and forgiveness help fulfill dreams for our lives?

Day 4: Along the Way, Remember These Things

I'm aware of the fact that I must be careful how I define a "winning life." In regard to dreaming, I could easily draw the conclusion that you're winning only if your dreams are being fulfilled. If they aren't, you're losing. This conclusion is far from true. Winning, as it relates to dreaming, is learning to wait on God for his timing, then executing your dream with biblical wisdom. There is both a God component and a man component involved. Fulfilling dreams involves both heavenly inspiration and earthly application. There is an undeniable ebb and flow with God-given dreams. And then there's living fully surrendered to him while learning to seize every moment. For me this has been the hardest lesson to learn while dreaming. I have to remind myself of a few things along the way.

Bad Beginnings Don't Mean Bad Endings

The movie *The Pursuit of Happyness*[1] tells the story of Chris Gardner. Christopher Paul Gardner's childhood was marked by poverty, violence, alcoholism, sexual abuse, and family illiteracy. He didn't even know his father and was taken away from his mother at a very tender age; he lived in foster homes for a large part of his childhood. He is now a CEO, investor, motivational speaker, author, and philanthropist. In fact, his book spent over twenty weeks on the *New York Times* best-seller list and has been translated into more than forty languages. You can see that, despite his unfortunate childhood, he didn't accept the fate he was handed. He took responsibility for his life and resolved to make a difference.

Chris's story is proof that bad beginnings don't mean bad endings. Think again about Joseph. The beginning of his dream started bloody—literally. When his brothers stripped his coat from his back, they covered it in blood and told their father a ferocious animal had eaten him. This coat, known as the coat of many colors, represented Jacob's favoritism toward Joseph, and it became the focal point of his brothers' hatred. Now this coat of many colors was covered in only one color—red. What a bloody beginning.

As believers, we must remember that Christ's blood, poured out at Calvary, covers our bloody beginnings. Our lives and dreams are continually made new in him; because of this fact, we have his favor on our lives.

Remember, up to this point Joseph was accustomed to the favor of an earthly dad who left him spoiled and egocentric. But the favor of God is different; it is his grace and mercy accomplishing in our lives what we could never do by ourselves. This favor leaves us humbled. And when his favor is there, regardless of how bloody our dreams or lives began, they can have a great ending.

Perhaps you've heard of the former prime minister of Great Britain, Winston Churchill. Churchill repeated a grade during elementary school, and when he entered the famous school at Harrow, he was placed in the lowest division of the lowest class. Later, he twice failed the entrance exam to the Royal Military Academy at Sandhurst. He was defeated in his first effort to serve in Parliament. He became prime minister at the age of sixty-two and later wrote, "Never give in, never give in, never, never, never, never—in nothing, great or small, large or petty—never give in except to convictions of honor and good sense. Never, Never, Never, Never give up"[2] (his capitals, mind you). The only way a bad beginning will have a great ending is if we never give in.

I Must Wear a Red Bandanna

Have you ever heard the story of the man with the red bandanna? It's the story of Welles Crowther, a true hero of the tragic day in America known as 9/11. As a child Crowther looked up to his father, and while watching his father prepare for work, he noticed him put a red bandanna in his pocket. Crowther asked why he did this, to which his dad responded, "Son, this red bandanna is my reminder to seize every moment in life and to remain willing, prepared, and able."

Later, his father gave him a red bandanna that would become his own keepsake and a link between father and son he would carry with him everywhere. Welles was seen wearing one under all his sports uniforms in high school and under his lacrosse helmet in college. In 1999 Crowther graduated with honors with a degree in economics. He subsequently moved to New York City, taking a job as an equities trader and settling into an office on the 104th floor of the World Trade Center's South Tower.

On September 11, 2001, minutes after United Airlines Flight 175 struck the South Tower between the seventy-seventh and eighty-fifth floors, twenty-four-year-old Crowther called his mother from his office at 9:12 a.m. He calmly left a brief message. "Mom, this is Welles. I want you to know that I'm OK." Crowther made his way down to the seventy-eighth floor sky lobby, where he encountered a group of survivors, huddled and waiting for help, including a badly burned Ling Young, who worked on the eighty-sixth floor in New York's Department of Taxation and Finance.

Young had been one of approximately two hundred people waiting at a bank of elevators to evacuate after the plane hit the tower, and she was one of the few survivors. Blinded by the blood covering her glasses, she was rescued when Crowther appeared, carrying a young woman on his back. He directed them in a strong, authoritative voice to the stairway, where the survivors followed him fifteen floors down. There he dropped off the woman he'd been carrying before heading back upstairs to assist others.

By the time he returned to the seventy-eighth floor, he had a bandanna around his nose and mouth to protect him from smoke and haze. As occupants of the tower headed for the street, Crowther turned around and went back inside multiple times, according to witnesses. He was last seen doing so with members of the New York Fire Department before the South Tower collapsed at 9:59 a.m. Many of the people he saved were reported as saying, "I was saved by the man in the red bandanna." Jefferson Crowther said of his son, "He didn't live long enough to be head of a corporation or do good works or endow a museum. But what he did on September 11, that's his legacy."

Welles Crowther left a legacy because he lived life ready to seize every moment, always willing, ready, and able. The red bandanna signified this life's motto. Though he never achieved the title of fireman or FBI agent, his name is mentioned along with names of other brave heroes of that historic day. Though his dream was never fulfilled, he lived with the qualities of a dreamer. In other words he didn't wait to "live" once his dreams were fulfilled; he lived with the qualities of a dreamer every day, and eventually he became a hero.[3]

I like to think that God has given us all a red bandanna and commissioned us to live with the same qualities. Joseph certainly did. He seized the moment to faithfully serve Potiphar even though he was a slave. Though falsely imprisoned, he would then be willing to serve the prison warden. He didn't allow bitterness of the moment to squelch his ability to interpret the cupbearer's dreams or to overlook the despondency of others. As a result he eventually became governor of a nation and the hero of millions. Whatever season he was in, he lived with a red bandanna in his pocket. We must do the same.

Eventually God Will Cause Me to Forget

There is something absolutely powerful embedded in the story of Joseph. First, his name means "add." Jacob and Rachel named him that because he was the next-to-last child added to Jacob later in his life. In the Old Testament names were important, and more often than not individuals grew into the character and nature of what their name meant. Joseph would increase in exceptional influence and responsibility throughout his lifetime. However, God used subtraction to bring this additional favor to his life.

Think about it. Joseph lost his family for seventeen years. Twice he lost his cloak. He ended up in prison and endured a time when he lost influence and experienced ineffectiveness. He was left with the feeling of being forgotten before he was finally delivered. But it was through this season of subtraction that maturity and wisdom were added to his life. God does the same with us. If I'm in a season of being stripped, it could be that I'm being equipped for a greater time in my life.

But there is something even more powerful than the meaning of Joseph's name and how he grew into its meaning. Joseph himself had two sons, and he summed up his entire journey through each of their names. The first son was Manasseh, a name that means "forget"; and the second son was Ephraim, a name that means "twice fruitful."[34] Listen to Joseph sum up his journey in Genesis 41:50–52. "Before the years of famine came, two sons were born to Joseph. Joseph named his firstborn Manasseh and said, 'It is because God has made me forget all my trouble and all my father's household.' The second he named Ephraim, 'It is because God has made me fruitful in the land of my suffering.'"

I don't know about you, but this story makes me tremble with wonder at God's ways. Here is a man, once sold as a slave, now saying that God caused him to forget the trouble he endured. Not only that, but God caused him to be fruitful in his long season of suffering.

I believe God does the same for you; in fact, he will bless you with fruitfulness in your life that will cause you to "forget" the hard things you had to walk through along the way. By forget I mean that those trials and difficulties don't leave you beaten up or burned out on God, your dreams, or even yourself. Isaiah 42:3 says, "A bruised reed he will not break, and a smoldering wick he will not snuff out."

We see a visual representation of this promise and the summary of Joseph's journey whenever Jacob, his father, would bless his sons Manasseh and Ephraim. By understanding Old Testament customs, we see that the oldest child was placed on the right-hand side of the patriarch and was blessed first with his right hand. But Jacob crossed his arms, causing the younger Ephraim to be blessed first because he'd placed his right hand on Ephraim and his left hand on Manasseh. Joseph even tried to talk Jacob out of doing this, but Jacob insisted. God was giving us a visual representation of his promises over our lives in the midst of the difficult process of dream development. Essentially, Jacob put fruitfulness ahead of forgetfulness at the conclusion of Joseph's long journey.

When all is said and done, after we've walked through the wilderness, spent time in the rock tumbler, and endured prison, I believe God brings us into such a season of fruitfulness that we "forget" the sting of the journey. This fruit might be "success" with our dream, or it could be that the manhood or womanhood forged in my life will cause me to rejoice for such fruit birthed in the desert. Either way, in the end I believe God will make the difficult walk, the heavy weariness, and the trying wilderness worth it. I believe he will have the final say, and I believe that one day, I will look back and define my journey by the fruit formed in my life, not by those things I would just rather forget. Thank God!

Conclusion

The story of Joseph consists of great reminders for us as we dream the dream God has given us. We must remain willing, able, and prepared. Like the man with the red bandanna, we must also be willing to seize the moment. Live life to the fullest today and trust God with tomorrow. We must also remember that regardless of the beginning, our dream can have a great God ending. Because of the blood of Jesus, his favor is with us when he births a dream in our hearts. And finally, don't become despairing but remember that in only a way God can, he can and will bring you into a time of such fruitfulness that you will "forget" the sting of the journey.

As you seek to live out your hinge decision, you must be faithful to remind yourself of these principles and other lessons along the way. Remember, God is gracious during the learning curve. In fact, sometimes dreams feel like one big life curve. But God is faithful and patient, and he extends grace to those willing to learn. I choose to remain willing. How about you?

How about You?

1. Would you describe your life or your dream as having a "bad beginning"? If so, has this beginning caused you to doubt the ending?

2. Do you live life with a red bandanna in your pocket? Do you embrace today and trust God with tomorrow? Are you generally a person who seizes every moment and remains willing, faithful, and able?

3. How do you feel about Joseph's statement that "God will cause me to forget"? Do you think God can do the same for you?

Day 5: Dream Disciplines

So far, we've looked at several disciplines from the life of Joseph. Some of the key disciplines we've talked about are the following:

- He chose a godly attitude in an ungodly atmosphere.
- He chose character at all costs. Though it cost him his cloak, he remained committed to his calling, kept his communion with God, and retained a sense of compassion for others.
- He was willing to serve the dream of someone else. Joseph interpreted Pharaoh's dream and was placed in charge of Egypt. By fulfilling these duties, his own dream was fulfilled. We must not underestimate the power of serving someone else. It may be through this service that our own dreams are fulfilled.

Today I would like to venture from my usual format and explore some other dream disciplines we might need to consider as well. These are merely snapshots of some disciplines that dreamers of the past and present embraced on the journey toward fulfillment. They serve as tried-and-true disciplines to consider as you strive to fulfill your own dreams.

Meaning, Not Just Money, Motivates Dreams

On day one of this week's reading, we discussed that one way to identify our dreams is by looking at our convictions. What deeply motivates us beyond those things on the surface, such as money, materialism, and notoriety? A great read for all dreamers and leaders is Simon Sinek's book *Start with Why*. The title alone is worth the price of the book. If a deep "why" guides our dreams, we will be more likely to execute all other disciplines of great dreamers and leaders. The truth is, great dreamers define their lives and dreams by core principles that often become a sense of purpose for their lives.

The "why" behind this book is twofold. First, the book is connected to a larger campaign designed to reach the unchurched. I simply don't know where I'd be (and its scary to even think about) if someone hadn't introduced me to Christ at the age of seventeen. This "why" guides my life, my ultimate dream, and certainly this book and campaign. Second, from the struggles I have personally endured and from the countless stories I've heard during my travels, I'm convinced more than ever that believers must understand how to live a life of biblical principles that produce the abundant life Jesus died for us to live. These two "whys" mean everything to me. Regardless of how many books or resources I sell, I'm going to strive to provide resources that help believers live an intentional life that influences others. What is the "why" (the meaning) behind your "what" (your dream)?

Dreamers Get Started by Setting Goals and Sticking to Them

Les Brown made two statements that particularly strike me:

- "You don't have to be great to get started, but you do have to get started to be great."
- "You will never be like the 'Little Engine That Could' if you sit around on your caboose."[2]

Proverbs 10:4 says, "Lazy hands make for poverty, but diligent hands bring wealth." Can you relate to the message behind these two quotes and this Bible verse? We must get started, and we must avoid laziness at all costs. For me getting started is usually the hardest part. Whether the start is related to my health, my dream, or even my day at times, getting started is tough. Can you relate?

One step I have taken is to institute a daily priority. The principle of a daily priority is the one thing on your to-do list you will absolutely do that day before going to bed. It is a nonnegotiable to-do item you will finish. Of course, this priority cannot be tasks like "Today I will write a book." But it could be "Today I will write two paragraphs if it kills me." Again, remember the concept of the hinge decision—only a small hinge is needed to open a huge door. The huge door is the big dream, the life overhaul, and the finished picture. The hinge is the small thing that can eventually open this huge door. For me, when I first started traveling and speaking, it was feast or famine. Either my voice mail was full with opportunities, or my phone didn't ring at all. Believe it or not, both scenarios made it easy for me to freeze. My decision was to determine to either make or return just one phone call a day. No exceptions. It had to be done. Each day, you must come up with a daily number-one priority as it relates to your dream and then do it. As I gain momentum with my number one, I can start exploring number two.

Dreamers Form Valuable Relationships

We cannot dream or fulfill our dreams alone. Who are the people in your life who are strategic in helping you fulfill your dreams? I'm convinced that we need at least three key relationships.

- Someone who inspires us to keep going. This is a "distant mentor." Dave Ramsey is mine. I've never met the man, but I'm inspired not only by the financial resources he has provided the world but by the way he runs his business. And because he's a writer and a business coach, I can glean from his business as I build my own. Who is your distant mentor?
- Someone who will hold my hand to the fire. I've already mentioned my friend Thomas. We meet every Wednesday morning at Starbucks. We ask each other the hard questions, update each other on our marriages, and then share what we are doing to build our businesses and ministries. Each week we tell each other three things we're going to do to move things forward in what we desire to become, instead of what we're doing just to maintain what we've always done. We're in two completely different lines of work, but we share the common desire to move forward.

- Someone already achieving what I want to do at a greater level. These aren't the Dave Ramseys of the world. These are people who are at a level or two just above your level. They are reachable with some effort on your part. They are the ones you ask for a phone call each quarter.

In the Bible even Jesus had his inner three (Peter, James, and John). In the world of discipling others, many Christian leaders suggest having a Paul (someone who disciples you), a Timothy (someone at your level of maturity), and a Barnabas (someone you are mentoring). In the world of business leadership, all material suggests key partnerships and relationships. Regardless of the arena your life and dream fall into, we need key people in our lives. Who are your three?

Dreamers Work Hard, Hard, and Harder—and Don't Quit

Discipline has often been defined as making yourself do the things you need to do, not the things you want to do. I once heard obedience defined as continued discipline in the same direction. Great dreamers and believers do both. They do the things they need to do, regardless of the way they feel. They put their hand on the plow and don't look back. They move forward and break up hard ground in front of themselves with God's help, even when they don't feel like doing so.

For dreams to come true, an undeniable amount of hard work and obedience must take place. When I first started writing, I heard about a successful writer who committed to writing one thousand words a day, regardless of how he felt. Not only that, but he tried to do so during the same two hours each day. I made an all-out commitment to do this, and I must admit that nine times out of ten this window of time fell when I least felt like writing. However, I pressed through and noticed something. Some of my best insight came the more I pressed through the initial "I don't feel like writing" mode. On some days I needed thirty minutes before the writing started to "click." On other days the "click" came in ninety minutes. And on other days the writing didn't click at all. But when it did click, especially on the heels of pressing through, some of my best writing was done. It was like God would squeeze out some deep stuff through this process, and he would reward me with his strength because my motives were pure. He will do the same for you.

Rose Blumkin founded Nebraska Furniture Mart, which Warren Buffet now owns. She worked every day at her store till the age of 103; she got "work sick" the only time she took a vacation for about a week. She knew the value of hard work. To become successful in life, you need to find what you love doing and do it with all your heart, even when you don't feel like doing anything at the moment.

Dreamers Are People Who Study Their Craft

Malcolm Gladwell popularized the idea that ten thousand hours of guided practice are the key to mastering a new skill or becoming an expert in certain areas.[3] That's about five years of forty-hour workweeks if I'm doing the math correctly. However, the question is, do I want to be successful enough at anything to really take the time to sharpen my own skill set?

Growing up, I loved watching Tony Gwynn hit a baseball. However, very few ever knew that Tony Gwynn, along with the best hitters in the major leagues, were disciplined students of the game and watched thousands of hours of tape to learn how to hit off opposing pitchers. The same is true about Peyton Manning, my favorite quarterback. I love his confidence under pressure, and his skill is superb. However, Peyton is also known as a student of the game who actually works harder off the field than he does on the field. The same was true of former boxer Mike Tyson. You thought Iron Mike was just a barbaric champion with theatrical stunts, but he was actually one of the best students of boxing to ever step into the ring. The list goes on and on, but the principle challenges me. Am I spending time as a student studying whatever skill I want to excel in or dream I want to fulfill in life?

Dreamers Don't Make Excuses—They Make Sacrifices

The great oil billionaire H. L. Hunt once said there are only two real requirements for success: first, he said, is to decide exactly what it is you want; second is to determine the price you are going to have to pay and resolve to pay that price.[4] The question is, am I willing to pay the price? Am I willing to stay up late and get up early? Am I willing to forgo that next episode on Netflix to spend time on my dream? Am I willing to get off Facebook to focus on something more productive I could be doing? These are just the small sacrifices I have personally asked myself to make. What about larger ones? Am I willing to rearrange my entire budget to save money so I can invest in my dream? Am I willing to take online classes at night to get the education I need? Am I willing to overhaul my health so I have greater energy throughout the day to put into my dream? These are the larger sacrifices.

Whether your sacrifices seem small or large, the bottom line is that dreamers don't make excuses—they make sacrifices. Everybody is busy; there isn't enough time in the day, and budgets are always tight. Welcome to the real world of dreaming! But it is through our sacrifices that our dreams become reality, and I must be willing to make them.

Dreamers Fail on Their Way to Success...Bottom Line

Lastly, remember that dreamers fail, and some of the best dreamers we have ever known endured great failure before they achieved great success.

- A newspaper editor fired Walt Disney because "he lacked imagination and had no good ideas." He went bankrupt several times before he built Disneyland. In fact the city of Anaheim rejected the proposed park on the grounds that it would attract only riffraff.

- Henry Ford failed and went broke five times before he succeeded.
- R. H. Macy failed seven times before his store in New York City caught on.
- Fred Smith, the founder of Federal Express, received a C on his college paper detailing his idea for a reliable overnight delivery service. His professor at Yale told him, "Well, Fred, the concept is interesting and well formed, but in order to earn better than a C grade, your ideas also have to be feasible."
- When Bell Telephone was struggling to get started, its owners offered all their rights to Western Union for $100,000. The offer was disdainfully rejected with the pronouncement, "What use could this company make of an electrical toy?"
- Here's what Apple computer founder Steve Jobs said about attempts to get Atari and HP interested in his and Steve Wozniak's personal computer. "So we went to Atari and said, 'Hey, we've got this amazing thing, even built with some of your parts, and what do you think about funding us? Or we'll give it to you. We just want to do it. Pay our salary, we'll come work for you.' And they said, 'No.' So then we went to Hewlett-Packard, and they said, 'Hey, we don't need you. You haven't got through college yet.'"
- Michael Jordan and Bob Cousy were each cut from their high school basketball teams. Jordan once observed, "I've failed over and over again in my life. That is why I succeed."
- Babe Ruth is famous for his past home run record, but for decades he also held the record for strikeouts. He hit 714 home runs and struck out 1,330 times in his career (about which he said, "Every strike brings me closer to the next home run").[5]

This list goes on and on, but the point is obvious. Failure is a breeding ground for success. So keep swinging the bat!

Conclusion

As we close out our week on Joseph, the dreamer, let's glean great encouragement and insight from his story. It is one like so many of our own. It is one of rising and falling, only to rise again. I'm determined to keep learning, keep growing, and keep applying the disciplines discovered in the lives of great men and women in the Bible and in history who refused to stop dreaming. Let the world say of you and me, "Here comes that dreamer!"

How about You?

1. What is one small thing you can start doing every day to start fulfilling your dream? Which of today's disciplines strike a chord with you the most?

2. What is at least one sacrifice you are willing to make?

3. Who is at least one person who will help you in some way fulfill your dream?

CHAPTER 6:

WEEK 6—MY DISCIPLINE

Day 1: Learning to Linger

Welcome to the sixth and final week of *A Life That Wins*. As you begin the sixth week of *A Life That Wins*, you have reason for celebration. You have made a hinge decision and are committed to seeing your decision become permanent. In conjunction with being a vital part of Reach the City and the 1–2–3 Challenge, you have had two discussions with your unchurched friend and personally witnessed the results of three days of community outreach. There's much to celebrate.

As we turn our attention to Week 6, we will look at our sixth and final destination of a life that wins. So far we've looked at decisiveness, drive, direction, dependency, and the willingness to dream. This week we explore discipline. I understand this word usually has a very negative connotation, but trust me—by the end of this week, you'll be craving it.

Let's jump right into a story that exemplifies discipline. It's another familiar story, the story of Joshua and the walls of Jericho found in Joshua 6. As you might remember, God delivered his people from Egyptian slavery and promised them rest in Canaan, a piece of land known as the promised land. However, there was a journey the Israelites had to undergo from Egypt to Canaan as they learned to trust in his protection and provision. This was a very difficult journey for this generation, and because of their unbelief and doubt, they never experienced this place of promise.

However, Joshua and his friend Caleb maintained trust and faith and were the only two who would have another shot at experiencing this much-awaited promise. Joshua became the leader of this second generation of Israelites and would have the incredible opportunity to feel this promised land beneath his feet. And he did so through discipline.

The first discipline Joshua exemplified took place long before we even get to the walls of Jericho in Joshua 6. It is revealed in the early life of Joshua, when he was an aide to Moses. Moses, as ruler of the Jewish people, met with God in a place called the Tent of Meeting. Joshua was found right beside this Tent of Meeting as Moses prayed and did something we must all learn to do from time to time.

Exodus 33:7–11 says,

> Now Moses used to take a tent and pitch it outside the camp some distance away, calling it the "tent of meeting."
>
> Anyone inquiring of the Lord would go to the tent of meeting outside the camp. And whenever Moses went out to the tent, all the people rose and stood at the entrances to their tents, watching Moses until he entered the tent. As Moses went into the tent, the pillar of cloud would come down and stay at the entrance, while the Lord spoke with Moses. Whenever the people saw the pillar of cloud standing at the entrance to the tent, they all stood and worshiped, each at the entrance to their tent. The Lord would speak to Moses face to face, as one speaks to a friend. Then Moses would return to the camp, *but his young aide Joshua son of Nun did not leave the tent.* (emphasis added)

Did you catch that? Joshua didn't leave the tent. He lingered in God's presence, fulfilling his responsibilities, then basking in and enjoying some extended time with God. This is something we must learn to do in today's world of busyness and hectic schedules, and it is a discipline much easier said than done. However, it is a much easier discipline to instill in our lives when we understand that God's presence boosts our character, builds our courage, and broadens our capacity.

Downloading an Upgrade

Let me back you up in the story and bring to your attention that Joshua had his name changed from Hoshea to Joshua. Keep in mind that God made name changes for a definite reason; a name change coincided with a life change to an entirely different person. The name Hoshea means "salvation," and the name Joshua means "God saves" or "God is salvation." The names are similar; however, the name Joshua carries with it a deeper, more personal, and specific level of trust. This might seem subtle, but it is a major upgrade in the character trait of trust.

Unlike Jacob, who needed a major character overhaul, Joshua simply needed his character to be upgraded to a higher level. It is true that there are areas of weakness in our lives that need a total transformation, but there are other areas that just need strengthening, upgrading, or improving.

I believe this upgrading takes place as we spend time (using a computer term) downloading the rich reality of God's presence in our lives. His presence makes our strengths even stronger and, like Hoshea, strengthens the godly character traits he is faithfully forming in our lives until they become our reputation or, better said, our new name.

This is important because Moses gives Hoshea this new name right before he is sent to spy out the promised land in Numbers 13:16. After the spies returned and gave their report of giants in the land, fear swept through the people like a plague except for Joshua and Caleb. Joshua, a man of God's presence, lived by his strengthened name and knew with certainty that God would fulfill his promise.

The Joshua kind of trust is cultivated as we spend time in the presence of God, because the awareness of his presence boosts our ability to trust him. As I spend time with him, trust is downloaded into my spirit; as a result, I become known as one who trusts the Lord with an unwavering loyalty.

Be Strong and Very Courageous

Unfortunately, Joshua and Caleb would have to wait several more decades to enter the promised land. Even though Joshua's name was strengthened, the faith of God's people was simply too weak, and unbelief was too prevalent for them to possess what God had promised.

After years had passed, there was a second opportunity for God's people to access Canaan through the entry point of Jericho with a march and a wall-tumbling shout. Right before they set out on their march, however, God told Joshua six times to be "strong and courageous." In fact, he told him to be strong and very courageous.

In *Living above the Level of Mediocrity*, Charles Swindoll tells a story by Bruce Larson that describes being strong and very courageous.

> When I was a small boy, I attended church every Sunday at a big gothic Presbyterian bastion in Chicago. The preaching was powerful and the music was great. But for me, the most awesome moment in the morning service was the offertory, when twelve solemn, frock-coated ushers marched in lock-step down the main aisle to receive the brass plates for collecting the offering. These men, so serious about their business of serving the Lord in this magnificent house of worship, were the business and professional leaders of Chicago. One of the twelve ushers was a man named Frank Loesch. He was not a very imposing-looking man, but in Chicago he was a living legend, for he was the man who had stood up to Al Capone. In the prohibition years, Capone's rule was absolute. The local and state police and even the Federal Bureau of Investigation were afraid to oppose him. But singlehandedly, Frank Loesch, as a Christina layman and without any government support, organized the Chicago Crime Commission, a group of citizens who were determined to take Mr. Capone to court and put him away. During the months that the Crime Commission met, Frank Loesch's life was in constant danger. There were threats on the lives of his family and friends. But he never wavered. Ultimately he won the case against Capone and was the instrument for removing this blight from the city of Chicago. Frank Loesch had risked his life to live out his faith. Each Sunday at this point of the service, my father, a Chicago businessman himself, never failed to poke me and silently point to Frank Loesch with pride.[1]

The type of courage displayed in this example as well as the kind of courage Joshua exemplified are cultivated in the presence of God. As I spend time with him, I'm spending time with his character, which as we've said boosts my own ability to trust in him. However, I also gain a deeper understanding of who he is because lingering in his presence gives birth to revelation.

Revelation isn't some weird and mystical term. No, daily revelation for the believer is simply spending time with God, knowing he is with us, and growing through the insight we glean while in his Word and in his presence. Revelation takes place when the Holy Spirit takes a verse you've read one thousand times and shows you something in a new a fresh way. And it is because of revelation that believers can declare, "God showed me something." This is when Christianity actually becomes intimate with the Father, Son, and Holy Spirit. We realize there is nothing like spending time with the one who created us and hearing him speak to our hearts.

The bottom line is that revelation keeps our relationship with God fresh. The apostle Paul understood this fact, which is why he prayed for the Ephesians a prayer you and I also need to pray often. Ephesians 1:17–20 says,

> I keep asking that the God of our Lord Jesus Christ, the glorious Father, may give you the Spirit of wisdom and revelation, so that you may know him better. I pray that the eyes of your heart may be enlightened in order that you may know the hope to which he has called you, the riches of his glorious inheritance in his holy people, and his incomparably great power for us who believe. That power is the same as the mighty strength he exerted when he raised Christ from the dead and seated him at his right hand in the heavenly realms, far above all rule and authority, power and dominion, and every name that is invoked, not only in the present age but also in the one to come.

You really should read those verses again—slowly. A million sermons could be written on this one passage, and the content of a million books wouldn't contain the measure of depth in this one prayer. Paul prayed that the eyes of the Ephesians' hearts would understand the incomparably great power for us who believe. This is the same power that raised Christ from the dead, the power that now lives and dwells in us. This is the same power, when deeply revealed and realized, that helps us to be not just courageous but very courageous.

Broadening My Capacity

Joshua was about to embark on a journey around the walls of Jericho that would stretch our modern-day faith to the breaking point. Sometimes the way God fulfills promises in your life, especially the timing in which he does so, will stretch your faith tremendously.

Have you ever felt as if Isaiah 54:2 could best describe your life? "Enlarge the place of your tent, stretch your tent curtains wide, don't hold back; lengthen your cords, strengthen your stakes." Right in the middle of this verse is one statement Joshua was challenged with, and you and I will also be challenged with it from time to time. "Don't hold back!" Joshua would have to do this as he marched around Jericho and held nothing back, trusting completely in God.

You and I must do this as we are being stretched and challenged to continue marching, even when we feel like we're at our limit. However, his presence broadens our capacity to fulfill what God is saying, because when we are stretched, we break into the realm of his unlimited resources. Spending time in the supernatural presence of God can give us faith to see the supernatural happening in and through our lives. The result is found back in the book of Ephesians 3:20. "To Him who is able to do exceedingly, abundantly, above all we can ask or imagine." In a couple of days, we will talk more about marching in faith in *A Life That Wins.* But for now please know this: when I spend time in his presence, God is magnified in my life, broadening my capacity to continue marching.

Conclusion

Following through on any hinge decision simply requires time in God's presence, time that will boost my ability to trust him, build my courage to take the first steps, and broaden my capacity to continue being faithful. However, we must understand that this hunger for God's presence must be cultivated in our lives. I heard it said once that hunger for God is like a sixth sense. You can taste, touch, smell, feel, and hear.

However, faith and hunger for God are the sixth sense that, unlike the first five, must be intentionally developed over time.

Just as we can cultivate a new taste for healthier foods, you can also cultivate a deep longing for the presence of God, but this will require discipline. As you practice his presence throughout the day and learn to spend extended time in prayer and worship, you will begin to thirst for God more and more (Ps. 42:6). My prayer for you has the words of Psalm 34:8—that you will taste and see that the Lord is good and that with each taste you will hunger more and more for the things of God in the days to come.

How about You?

Instead of asking you three questions at the end of today's reading, as I have done throughout this book, I'm asking you today to fulfill two challenges to help you incorporate the discipline of each day's reading.

The first challenge is to decide what you are going to do for a regular time with God for at least three days a week from this point forward. Are you going to use the SOAP Bible study method we've talked about? Where will you continue to read the Bible at the conclusion of this week, and what items will you pray about daily? Again, strive to form a plan for three to five meaningful times a week that last fifteen to thirty minutes. Basically, you are answering the question "What am I doing next for my quiet times?" after you finish this forty-day challenge.

Next, schedule extended time with God and learn to linger. Choose one discipline from the following list or challenge yourself with all three.

- Listen to praise and worship music on your way to and from work for one week.
- Give yourself a sixty-minute personal prayer and worship time that you schedule with God on your calendar each month. This is above and beyond your daily time with God. This is an appointment with God that you don't miss, not even for a doctor's appointment, a meeting with your boss, or one of your kids' athletic events. It's a nonnegotiable meeting time that cannot be changed or rescheduled.
- In the next forty days, tithe your time with God for just one day. There are twenty-four hours in a day, so that's 144 minutes with God. Select a Christian book to read, a book in the Bible to study, and a favorite worship CD to sing; then linger in God's presence.

Day 2: A Man's Best Friend

It's been said that a dog is a man's best friend. I couldn't disagree more, at least in my situation. I have a dog named Sophie that I promise you is mentally challenged. She is half Maltese and half poodle. I call her a mutt. My kids call her a designer dog. Either way, she's no best friend to me. She wakes us up early, barks in response to anything, and is incredibly needy. True, she's still a puppy, but I doubt she will grow into my best friend. That deep-down loyalty, that willingness to protect me at all costs, and that close companionship dog lovers boast about just aren't there yet.

On the other hand, Joshua could relate to having a true friend who was deeply loyal, would protect him at all costs, and remained a close companion for years to come. His name was Caleb, and guess what his name meant? "Mighty dog." How's that for irony? The name Joshua, as we read yesterday, means "God is salvation." They seem like an uncommon pairing of names for such a noble task as possessing the promised land. However, their relationship reveals the power of biblical friendship and true accountability marked by loyalty, safety, and companionship.

Yesterday I encouraged you to maintain your time with God and even learn to linger in his presence beyond this forty-day journey. Today I'm asking you to maintain the second key discipline threaded throughout this book. Remain involved in an accountable relationship with someone who, like Caleb, is a mighty dog—loyal, trustworthy, and willing to protect you and pray for you with unwavering friendship.

We discover the nature of Joshua and Caleb's relationship in Numbers 13 as part of Joshua's story. Here Moses sends twelve spies into the land of Canaan to see whether it was everything God had promised. It certainly was and so much more. However, it was a land not only flowing with milk and honey but also filled with giants and some fierce enemies who would have to be defeated. Joshua and Caleb were two of the twelve spies, and upon their return to Moses, the other ten began to spread a bad report about the land, inciting fear in the hearts of God's people.

Caleb spoke in Numbers 13:30. "We should go up and take possession of the land, for we can certainly do it." I don't know about you, but that's the kind of guy I want on my team. In fact, I want an accountability partner who sees the fruit, not just the fight. I want an accountability partner whose life is harnessed in faith, not in fear. And I want someone who not only will march with me but also isn't afraid to stake claim on the promises that rightfully belong to us in Christ Jesus. I realize these are high standards, but as you and a friend commit to an accountable relationship, these are qualities for both of you to develop over time.

Fight or Fruit?

In the promised land there were giants known as the Amalekites who were fierce fighters and protectors of their land. For the Israelites to possess this promised land, they would have a good fight on their hands. However, there was also amazing fruit there. While scouting the land, the spies visited a place called Eschol to determine whether Canaan was a fertile and fruit-producing land. To their amazement they found grapes so big that two clusters had to be carried on a pole between two men. Now that's big fruit! However, the moment they reached Moses, they dropped this visible representation of God's blessing to the ground and began complaining about the fight instead of complimenting the fruit.

Can you track where I'm going with this? The fruit lay on the ground, while the other ten spies filled the Israelites with fear and worry. Joshua later spoke up, stating, "The land we passed through and explored is exceedingly good." But at that point, it was too late. The fear of the fight became bigger than the reality of the fruit.

One characteristic you can seek in an accountability partner is someone who sees the fruit, not just the fight—someone who will remind you why the battle is worth it and helps you to focus on the job to be done and on the joy that lies ahead of you when the job is completed; someone who will believe with you that the journey, though it may be difficult, will be worth it; someone who will hold your hand to the fire when the battle rages hot.

As you meet with your accountability partner from this point forward, one exercise I would strongly recommend is for each of you to paint a picture of the fruit that lies ahead. In other words look at where you are now and dream together about what could be. Dream a little bit about what your business could look like at the next level or what your relationship with your spouse or kids could look like with a little (or a lot) of work. Tell each other why you desire to keep your finances in order and what your future could look like without debt. A good order to start with is to dream about the fruit, engage in the fight, and keep remembering the fruit. Remember from Week 2 that David was driven not only by reverence but also by rewards.

Faith or Fear?

Not only do you want an accountability partner who sees the fruit instead of the fight; you want someone whose life in general is rooted in faith, not in fear. This isn't to say you shouldn't share life with someone who battles with fear. It *is* to say that both of you should have a mutual agreement that you will be more centered on faith in God and his word than on your natural fear. Otherwise your relationship could turn into "misery loves company" instead of company that spurs courage.

This was the case for Joshua and Caleb's lives. Again, look at Joshua's response to the unbelief of the other ten spies and the budding doubt in all the Israelites. Joshua said in Numbers 14:8–9, "If the Lord is pleased with us, he will lead us into that land, a land flowing with milk and honey, and will give it to us. Only don't rebel against the Lord. And don't be afraid of the people of the land, because we will swallow them up. Their protection is gone, but the Lord is with us. Don't be afraid of them."

Wow, talk about a different perspective! The doubting ten saw only bad circumstances from their own perspective. Joshua and Caleb saw their lives and circumstances from God's perspective. The troubled ten saw only what they could do or, more accurately, what they couldn't do. The terrific two saw what God could do. Put simply, Joshua and Caleb remembered what I call "the God factor."

I want and need someone in my life who will remember the God factor. In other words I want an accountability partner who reminds me not only of what I should be doing but also of what God has already done and what he can do. I need accountability to do my part, but I also need to be reminded of God's part. In fact, I want someone who will constantly remind me to do my small part as God does his big part.

This, my friend, is someone rooted in faith, not fear. Later God would describe Caleb as one who would be allowed into the promised land because he possessed a "different spirit." While others were driven by despair, he was driven by destiny. While others lived by fear, he lived by faith. And while others were seeing only the giants in the land, he was seeing his giant God. I want to have his spirit. And I want to link arms with someone who shares the same. "For God has not given us a Spirit of fear, but of love, power, and soundness of mind" (2 Tim. 1:7).

In this day and time, anyone can easily live in a spirit of fear. But I choose to walk with those who have a different spirit—one of power, love, and a soundness of mind.

Now Give Me My Mountain!

Caleb would march with Joshua around the walls of Jericho. He circled with Joshua thirteen times in seven days. Around and around they went, spirits high, knowing that this was finally "it." But still they walked in sync and fulfilled the commands God had given them. Let me get to the point quickly on this one. An accountability partner is someone who circles with us. He or she puts one foot in front of another and simply walks by our side. And just like Joshua and Caleb walked around the same walls several times before the walls fell, an accountability partner understands that it's going to take some time for hinge decisions, growth, and character development to become permanent in our lives. They are patient *and* persistent. They are compassionate, but at the same time they challenge us to contend for our faith and keep walking until walls fall. They know when to cry with us but also when to slap us on the rear end and tell us to keep walking.

After circling Jericho and after the initial process of possessing the promised land unfolded, Caleb looked at Joshua and said, "Now give me my mountain." (Josh. 14:12)

God promised Caleb a portion of the promised land because of his different spirit, and finally Caleb, now much older in years, boldly and plainly said, "Now give it to me!"

Boy, I love that boldness. There Caleb was, having waited decades for this promise to come to pass, willing to now stake a claim to what was rightfully his. Remember, his name means "mighty dog." And now it appears that he wasn't just a dog but a bulldog. As I heard it once said, the reason a bulldog has a flat face is so that he can latch onto something and be able to maintain his ability to breathe even while refusing to let go. I want to be that kind of believer, and I want to live life with people who are willing to claim the promises of God and not let go. I want someone who will inspire me to lock my teeth into God's truth and refuse to believe any lie of the enemy.

Conclusion

Who is the Caleb in your life? Who is the one who will see the fruit, not just the fight? Who is the one whose life is harnessed by faith, not fear? Who possesses that "different spirit"? And who is the one who will tenaciously be a constant reminder of the truth of God's word?

Who will inspire you to sink your teeth into the promises of God and not let go?

This kind of person can be hard to find, I admit. So if you feel like the Calebs of the world are few and far between, I completely understand. However—and this is a big "however"—if you want a Caleb in your life, you must be willing to be this kind of individual for someone else. Remember my opening illustration about my dog Sophie? Animal behaviorists would say that Sophie's behavior as she develops is largely based on my behavior toward her. In other words a man's best friend isn't born overnight but developed over time. The same is true with accountable friendships. I must be willing to be this type of friend to someone else and trust that a Joshua-Caleb friendship will grow over time.

The bottom line is this: we cannot wait to find someone who carries these qualities. We must strive to possess them ourselves and trust that God will help identify this type of person in our lives. And as we seek the Lord for the "right" person to appear, we might want to make ourselves available to individuals who have committed to overcoming life-controlling issues or maybe to a younger person in the church who needs encouragement or mentoring at his or her time of life. Encouraging him or her will foster the growth of Caleb qualities in your own life—and who knows what impact you might have on each other? The Calebs are out there, and I believe you are committed to becoming one of them.

How about You?

My challenge to you after this forty days is to find an accountability partner whom you meet with at least once every two weeks from this point forward.

I know many of you will continue to attend a small group through your church after this series is over. However, an accountability relationship is different. It's more personal and therefore carries greater potential for significant impact in your life. Therefore, in the next ten days ask someone to be your Caleb. Set two appointments with this individual in the next thirty days. And in your first meeting, reread this day's reading and explore together whether the two of you can fit the description of an accountability partner as described in today's reading. Then start circling walls together and staking out your rewards.

Day 3: Just Keep Walking

My favorite animated movie of all time is *Finding Nemo.* It is brilliantly written, funny, and inspiring. It is also actually full of life lessons you could write an entire book about. The best lesson, in my view, comes from Dory. Dory is Marlin's newfound friend, a friend he has a love-hate relationship with while on his journey to find his lost son, Nemo. In a moment when Marlin is already stressed to the core, Dory (who is "different," to say the least) breaks out in song. You will probably remember the famous line from her song: "Just keep swimming. Just keep swimming, swimming, swimming, swimming.

What a profound life principle. Just keep swimming! For our lives and for Joshua and Caleb the saying only needs a little modification. "Just keep walking." Like Joshua and Caleb, keep walking and walking and walking and walking. And like Marlin, we need to get that stuck in our heads. Actually, we need to get that stuck in our spirits.

God gave Joshua the instructions (in chapter 6) to circle the walls of Jericho once a day for six days and on the seventh day to walk around it seven times before giving a loud shout. Needless to say, there are many thoughts about the reasoning behind this war strategy. Whatever the case, it didn't change the fact that Joshua was called to walk and walk and walk. His part was to keep walking, and our part is to do the same.

We must walk when the devil stalks, walk when doubters talk, and walk when the flesh talks back.

When the Devil Stalks, We Must Continue to Walk!

Anytime we start striving to walk hard after God, the devil doesn't like it. There's no escaping the reality of the very real enemy we have called "the devil" who has come to steal, kill, and destroy (John 10:10). First Peter 5:8 declares that he's like a roaring lion, looking for someone to devour. He, the father of lies, is looking to quench the life we can have in Jesus Christ.

Part of his strategy is to come against us when we are the weakest. This is what prowling lions do when they are on a hunt. Lions that are ferociously hungry are equally methodical and deliberate in their attack on prey as they wait for a weaker animal to fall behind the rest of the pack. When an animal becomes weak and isolated, they become an easy target for the lion and, more times than not, dinner.

In my opinion two of the most common times the devil comes against us is when we are weak or when we're trying to become strong. On one hand we are easy targets; on the other, we pose a serious threat. Either way, when he stalks, we must continue to walk.

When we are weak, we must continue to lean on the strength of others and on our accountability partner. We must also remain committed to attending church. Hebrews 10:25 makes it clear that we aren't to forsake assembling together. This isn't just so our pastor can claim us as a number on the church attendance roll. It's because there are spiritual strength and encouragement we are infused with when worshiping collectively. But when we become isolated, we become targets.

Likewise, any time we take steps to become aggressive in our faith, the enemy takes a step toward us. You might have already noticed this as you took the 1–2–3 Challenge and began reaching out to an unchurched person. Do you realize that when you are trying to reach out to someone else, you are reaching into enemy territory? You and I certainly don't like our home being broken into or a stranger trespassing on our property, and neither does the enemy. Take a radical step toward God and reaching others, and the enemy will take a step against you to protect what he's claimed as his own.

At this point you and I have a decision to make when it comes to engaging in spiritual conflict. Either we can become intimidated and shrink back, or we can claim Hebrews 10:6, which says we aren't of those who shrink back and are destroyed, but we believe God and are saved. Either we can cower in the corner and hope to escape spiritual battery, or we can rise up and realize that reaching someone unchurched and growing spiritually is worth the battle. We can quit, or we can keep walking. I choose to keep walking and walking and walking. And if I should find myself flat on my face, I will call on God's grace, stand up, and start walking again.

When Doubters Talk, We Must Continue to Walk

Joshua and Caleb were familiar with the doubters. As we saw yesterday, there were ten spies who bred contempt and doubt into tens of thousands of the first-generation called to possess the promised land. However, can we look at doubt from a slightly different angle today? I realize doubt from others is very direct, like with the doubting ten. There are some who will mock, make fun, and directly doubt our attempts to live radically for God. Whether it be through rolling their eyes when we declare our dream or looking at us with awkward silence, there will be times when direct doubt will strike our hearts, and we must simply choose to keep walking.

However, one form of doubt might take place within your own immediate family. For parents who have made hinge decisions together and have committed to the 1–2–3 Challenge, kids whose parents are now trying to implement change in the home may express some doubt. By doubt, I mean uncertainty that could be expressed when the former commonplace becomes questioned.

For example, parents who have decided to limit the amount of time their kids spend on electronics might catch some flack, to say the least. To navigate the decision, parents will have to spend time with their kids, explaining their reasoning and then helping them redirect their behavior to other things. This will demand some walking on the part of the parents. The same could be true of the couple trying to get their finances in order. If they have decided to stop eating out so much, they must have a conversation with their children to explain the reasoning behind the decision and the benefits of eating around the kitchen table together. We must remember that change naturally breeds a level of uncertainty. But as we continue to walk together and *explain* the unknown as best we can, this uncertainty will be greatly reduced, and others in our family will embrace the change.

Finally, I realize that there will be some scenarios where one spouse has committed to living a biblical life and the other has not. This situation can be very difficult, often demanding that you tread lightly and walk patiently as a believer. The best answer is the principle found in 1 Peter 3:1–2. "Wives, in the same way be submissive to your husbands so that, if any of them do not believe the word, they may be won over without words by the behavior of their wives, when they see the purity and reverence of your lives." I believe this verse can apply to both men and women. There are times in life when we must win others in our home with our behavior before trying to win them with our words. We must commit to walk out Scripture as best we can. Let's not become frustrated, because then we could push others away with our words. Let's focus on our own faith, enjoy our relationship with Christ, and win spouses over time with our continuing walk with God.

We Must Keep Walking When Our Flesh is Back Talking

Walking when our flesh is talking back is a different kind of challenge. By talking back, I mean that our flesh often doesn't die easily. It's kind of like telling our kids to do something they really don't want to do, and they give every reason not to do what we are requesting. It's so annoying to us who are parents because talking back undermines our authority and is very disrespectful toward our expressed desires as parents. But believe it or not, the greatest talk backers in our lives are not our children. They are our flesh.

The flesh is that side of us that is still being renewed daily in Christ. It's that part of our minds that is still carnal and competes with our spiritual desires. It's that part of us that desires comfort when the cross is calling for commitment. It's that part of us that tells us to stop when our spirit tells us to go. It's a daily battle we all face, which is why Paul said he had to choose daily to die to self.

But the flesh is also where our own doubts and limiting beliefs lie. In this arena of conflict, it's not the voice of the devil, nor anybody else for that matter, that keeps us from moving forward in an aggressive faith. It's simply our own thoughts and our own voices.

- "I can't do this thing called 'radically living for God.'"
- "Who do I think I am?"
- "I have messed this thing up more times than I have succeeded."
- "I still have too many regrets from the past to seize my present." The list can go on and on, but such statements are "limiting beliefs." They are beliefs that, just as they are called, limit us from fully striving for greater things with God. We all have them, and they can fiercely talk back when we are trying to crucify them. They undermine our authority in Christ and Christ's authority in us. They disrespect the very spiritual desires we have to move forward into greater levels with God. And they can be very detrimental because limiting beliefs will ultimately limit our behavior—which is what discipline is all about.

The answer? You got it—keep walking when the flesh is back talking. Take those thoughts captive as you keep moving your feet forward. Recognize the limiting beliefs, resist the lies behind them, renew your mind through God's word, rejoice that you are his, and resolve to live with a persevering and growing faith.

Conclusion

Growing in our faith isn't an easy process, and we will surely face the enemy, our flesh, our own doubts, and the doubt of others. And when we do, we have a decision to make. Do we stop or keep going? Do we settle, or do we refuse to stop? And do we withdraw our efforts, or do we choose to keep walking? I choose to just keep swimming—I mean, walking. It's a principle that, like Marlin said, needs to get stuck in our heads and in our hearts.

How about You?

Today's discipline is really best defined as the discipline of preserving faith. We saw it in Week 1 when Jonathan and his young armor-bearer refused to stop halfway to the enemy's camp.

We saw it in Week 2 when David ran to the battle line to meet Goliath. We saw it in Week 3 when Leah had to continue to persevere through different levels of freedom. We saw it in Week 4 when Jacob had to learn dependency in a very long journey, and we saw it in Week 5 when Joseph had to remember God, even when he was thrown into a pit and then into prison. And most importantly, we are called throughout Scripture to keep growing in our faith.

Your assignment this week is to identify the one enemy in your life that keeps your feet from moving forward. Take time to pray about this issue, share it with your accountability partner, and come up with a strategy that will keep you moving forward. Review the five Rs in Week 2 and become determined to keep walking and walking and walking.

Day 4: The Silence Is Deafening

You might have heard or even used the popular phrase "the silence is deafening." This expression means a lack of response that reveals something significant. Silence is actually a great tool of communication. How many times do moms and dads just stare at a misbehaving child to get his or her attention? Teachers are actually taught this technique to grab the attention of an unruly classroom. When I was a youth pastor, my students would tell me that I had a certain look that was far more effective at grabbing their attention than trying to shout above them. Silence, when used properly, is actually captivating, and it's a great way to bring attention and focus to something more significant.

This was actually the technique used to defeat Jericho. The Lord gave instructions to march around the city once a day for six days and on the seventh day to march around it six times with the priests blowing the trumpets. Upon hearing the trumpets sound a long blast, the Israelites were to give a loud shout, and then the walls would fall. However, all the marching up to the trumpet blast was to be done in silence. In Joshua 6:10, Joshua commanded the army, "Don't give a war cry, don't raise your voices, and don't say a word until the day I tell you to shout. Then shout!"

It's easy to focus on the shout of the seventh day and fail to mention the silence of the first six days. Today the focus of our reading is more about personal worship and the silence of the six days than about the shout on the seventh. I like to compare the six days in this story to my life of worship during the week and the seventh day to my public worship on Sundays. For six days I choose to live a life of worship, often obeying God silently with no fanfare and often when no one is looking. Our life of worship demonstrates that our attention and focus are on something more significant in our lives—his presence. And then on the seventh day, I have the opportunity to express corporate celebration of the God whom I serve.

Yesterday we looked at persevering in faith, walking with the Lord, and not giving up. Today we're going to look at our walk with the Lord as a life of personal worship. As you know, living a life of worship and obedience requires personal discipline.

This is often where the rubber meets the road when it comes to our faith and where the word *discipline* conjures up the negativity usually attached to it. However, we can embrace discipline, obedience, and wisdom when we really understand a few principles. First, discipline is the pathway from our "here" to our "there." Second, we must understand discipline's domino effect. And third—and this is a big one—discipline is more about God's yes than God's no.

From My "Here" to My "There"

We will be less likely to shun the idea of discipline if we come to realize that discipline is the pathway from where we are to where we want to be. Remember, in Week 1 we talked about the before and after pictures companies use when promoting a special workout or health-related product. It's the after picture that usually motivates us to pick up the phone and order the product. However, daily discipline is what transforms the before picture into the after picture. This is the case for every area of our lives: physical, emotional, financial, relational, and of course spiritual.

This is an easy concept to write about and one we would all agree with. However, walking out daily discipline in our lives can be tough. For starters, our "here" can seem a long way from our "there." Second, the road of discipline can be lonely. Although we should be like the Israelites, willing to march silently unto the Lord, let's face it; this walk can sometimes feel lonely.

And third, if we don't carry out discipline in our lives the right way, we can feel overwhelmed, give up, and end up feeling like a big failure. This is where learning to set goals becomes so important. Goals keep our discipline on track and moving forward on our way to our "there," whatever "there" might look like.

Here are some tips to make good goals. They will look familiar to you because they are the same ones you read about on Day 1 when you were developing your first hinge decision. Let them serve again as a structure for making new goals beyond the conclusion of this forty-day campaign.

- Good goals start when you're being honest with yourself. I fly in and out of airports frequently. Early on in my travels, there were often short layovers at airports, and my next plane would take off at the other end of the airport. When you get off at one terminal, there is usually a map of the airport that has a big, fat, highlighted arrow that says, "YOU ARE HERE." Once I'm able to locate where I am, I can determine the best way to catch my next flight. In the same way, to reach your ultimate destination, you must accurately assess where you are. Be honest with yourself and your accountability partner. From this honesty you will find that the Holy Spirit is able to chart the most effective path to reaching where and who you really want to be.
- Good goals are specific. Don't just say, "I want to lose weight." Say instead, "I want to lose thirty pounds."
- Good goals are measurable. It isn't enough to say, "I'm going to lose thirty pounds." You must say, "I'm going to lose two pounds a week for fifteen weeks."
- Good goals have a time frame and deadline. "I'm going to lose two pounds a week for fifteen weeks from January 1 to March 15."
- Good goals prioritize planned behaviors and benchmark behaviors. "I'm going to lose two pounds a week for fifteen weeks from January 1 to March 15. I'm going to do so by counting my calories each day and not eating more than eighteen hundred calories in a twenty-four-hour period." Now that is planned behavior. However, setting a reasonable deadline to lose a certain amount of weight and planning your behavior are one thing. Setting a deadline to improve your marriage is

a bit tougher. However, you can set a deadline to start engaging what I call "benchmark behaviors." A benchmark behavior to improve your marriage could be, "In three months time, my wife and I will have established the habit of going on a date together at least once every two weeks." By hitting this benchmark, you are more likely to achieve your overall goal of improving your marriage.

- Good goals are incentivized. We don't need to wait to celebrate until the final outcome is accomplished. We need to celebrate along the way. Reward yourself. "When I lose ten pounds, I'm going to treat myself to a new outfit."
- Good goals are written down. I know it would be easy to type them out or punch them into a note on your mobile phone. However, Chris Hogan, team member in the Dave Ramsey organization, suggests handwriting them on a card, laminating the card, and keeping it on your person through the entire year.[1] His point is well made. We all have dozens of notes in our mobile phones that we never look at and dozens of e-mails we've sent ourselves that we've not even opened. If your goals are that important to you, do something different with them. Handwrite them and carry your laminated card with you in your pocket. Let the card serve as a reminder and a form of accountability throughout the year.

These five guidelines are good points to remember as you establish goals that will help you achieve discipline from your "here" to your "there." Once you establish goals along the way, you will experience the domino effect.

The Domino Effect

I'm sure you've either played dominoes or seen them fall one after another. The hard part is lining them all up. The easy part is pushing the first one and watching them all fall. It's amazing that what takes several hours to set up can all fall in a matter of seconds.

This is how I view discipline. The hardest part of discipline is getting ready to actually make the decision and getting started. However, once we do and we have made good goals to strive for along the way, the dominoes can actually fall pretty quickly one after the other. In other words we can start seeing good benefits from our discipline which gives us the motivation to keep going. Once an area of our lives starts showing improvement, we become ready to see the next phase completed and the next and the next.

When my wife was pregnant with our first child, she gained the expected weight as any woman should. However, so did I. I thought I was being a good husband, but long after she lost her baby weight, I still had mine. Then my travel schedule picked up to new levels, my eating patterns became more irregular, and what started as a nine-month sympathy gain became nine years. Finally, it became time to do something about my weight problem. (It's funny how long we know we *ought* to do something before actually doing something.) For me starting was the hardest part. I had the plan in place (all dominoes lined up), but pushing over that first domino was difficult. However, once I started, within a matter of a couple of weeks I could begin telling a difference. This change spurred on my discipline and actually caused me to want to learn more about health because the benefit of how I felt was so drastic. Once I made the initial push, there was no stopping the benefits.

The domino effect essentially means that discipline will give birth to more discipline in our lives as our march around the walls of Jericho begins to pay off. It has been said that forming a new habit takes twenty-one days. However, I believe, with many areas of life, that if we would do something differently for just three days straight, we could begin to notice a difference that would cause dominoes to start falling quickly.

Within three days, most people could lose at least one pound of weight. Within three days of eating at home for lunch, most people could still see $15 to $30 in their wallets on day four. Within three days of sowing intentional love into that coworker or boss who gets on your nerves, you could start noticing a shift in their attitude toward you. And within three days of getting up just thirty minutes earlier and spending time with God, you will notice a huge difference in your stress level by the end of the third day. Just give something three days of intentional discipline, and I bet you'll start desiring to stick with it the fourth day and beyond. But you must get started.

Discipline Is More about Preserving Relationships Than Following Rules

Right at the center of Joshua's march was the presence of God. The silence of the Israelites was, in part, out of reverent worship for the God they had with them. For you and me as New Testament believers, we carry the very presence of God in our lives. Paul tells us in 1 Corinthians 10:31, "Whatever you do, do for the glory of God." This means that both our obeying and even fulfilling a goal we believe God is leading us in should be done ultimately to strengthen the relationship we have with him. Christianity is first about our relationship, and the "rules" serve only as a means to grow in our personal worship.

This is why once we get to Joshua 7, we see God asking Joshua to take extreme measures against Achan and his family. Achan kept for himself some of the plunder linking him to the worship of false gods. After being confronted, he and his family were stoned to death. This might seem extreme for some. Others might say, "Yeah, but that was the Old Testament." Then turn to Acts 5, and you'll see a similar story unfold about Ananias and Sapphira.

Right after the walls of Jericho fell in the Old Testament and after the church was birthed in the New Testament, God made a point about sin. We cannot expect to experience a full measure of God's presence and blessing if we are welcoming any kind of compromise in our lives. Scripture is clear that "a little yeast works through the whole batch of dough" (Gal. 5:9). Just a little bit of sin can become a big deal, and even bad company can corrupt good character (1 Cor. 15:33). If we want the full measure of John 10:10 in our lives, we must make sure the small stuff doesn't become big and quench the Holy Spirit in us (1 Thess. 5:19). Compromise can be the biggest enemy of full measure.

Joshua was commanded to ensure that God's people worshiped the only true God by eliminating false gods from the land. Otherwise the people would begin to mix the two and fall into idolatry. In the New Testament the Holy Spirit was poured out on the disciples, empowering them to be the church. They had the responsibility we still have to this day, which is not to quench or grieve the Holy Spirit (Eph. 4:30; 1 Thess. 5:19) but to keep our spiritual fervor, serving the Lord (Rom. 12:11).

This might sound extreme, but once I realize that by taking drastic measures against sin I'm actually protecting the full measure of God's presence and power in my life, then my perspective totally changes. I want everything God has for me, and I must be willing to do anything and everything necessary to preserve my relationship with him. Remember, in Week 2, we talked about David's cutting off Goliath's head to ensure what came against God's people was good and dead. I must be willing to do the same, and I'm more willing to do so when I realize it's about growing the best relationship with God possible, not just about following rules. I want him at the very center of my life and nothing else.

Conclusion

Discipline isn't easy, but the rewards are amazing. Discipline transforms us from our "here" to our "there." Once I push over the first domino, look out, because very soon the benefits of discipline will start spurring me on to further action. And my relationship with God serves as my primary goal for any measure of discipline I take.

Then I will continue to experience everything he has for me. Joshua and the priests marched around the walls in silence, drawing their attention and everyone else's attention to the one true God. I ultimately choose to view discipline as my way of doing the same.

How about You?

From this point forward, what is your next hinge decision? In what area of your life would you like to achieve another level of discipline? Spend some time charting out your "here to there" strategy. What are some goals you can establish along the way to ensure that you will keep striving toward your desired destination?

Day 5: As for Me and My House

Welcome to the final day of this forty-day challenge! Today we end with the one thing I believe should always be on our minds: our families. In fact, throughout this book I've mentioned the family background of all the biblical characters we've studied. More specifically, I've talked about how each family's faith, or lack thereof, significantly impacted the characters' stories.

The same is absolutely true for our lives. My faith as a parent has a tremendous impact on the faith of my children. Joshua understood his faith would in some way, either for good or bad, play a major role in the unfolding story of his children. This is why in Joshua 24, long after the walls fell and as the people of God were once again flirting with foreign gods, he made the statement that defined his legacy. Joshua 24:15 says, "As for me and my house, we will serve the Lord."

This one verse is displayed in millions of Christian homes around the world. And though it's a great verse to hang on the wall, it's a verse that is difficult to live out in today's world. Life is busy. Children and teenagers have a mind of their own. The culture is becoming more ungodly by the minute. And parenting is just plain hard.

However, I believe you and I can parent the next generation in a godly way. I believe we can raise our children to rise above the norm. And I believe we can see the cross of Jesus Christ and his empty grave as the center of our children's lives in the midst of a godless culture. I don't know about you, but when I die, I would like my children and grandchildren to be able to inscribe my epitaph with the words of Joshua 24:15.

It's never too early to start dreaming about the legacy you want to leave behind for your family or future family. And it's never too late to reclaim a biblical, positive, and healthy legacy in a home that has become sidetracked. I tell parents and teenagers in our parent/teen conferences across the nation that it's never too early or too late to declare, "As for me and my house, we will serve the Lord."

In today's reading I would like to offer starter information I share in the parent/teen conference. This information is based on Joshua 24:15, cited above, and on Deuteronomy 6:4–6: "Hear, O Israel: The Lord our God, the Lord is one. Love the Lord your God with all your heart and with all your soul and with all your strength. These commandments that I give you today are to be on your hearts. Impress them on your children. Talk about them when you sit at home and when you walk along the road, when you lie down and when you get up. Tie them as symbols on your hands and bind them on your foreheads. Write them on the doorframes of your houses and on your gates."

These two passages can serve as a framework for biblical parenting. So as we close out this book with your children in mind, remember to teach them a few things about discipline (about living daily for the Lord). First, teach them that discipline is more about God's yes than God's no. Second, as a parent, remember to establish common ground to connect your children to Christ. And third, learn to disciple your children along the way.

Discipline Is More about God's Yes Than God's No

Perhaps you've heard one of the following statements or said one of them yourself:

- "Mom, can I stay out past curfew?"
- "Mom, can you drop me off at the mall for three hours so I can hang out with my friends?"
- "Dad, can I have an extra twenty dollars above my allowance?"

The list of questions any parent will hear in his or her lifetime is breathtaking. Some questions are easy to answer, and others are more difficult. But at some point, we will tell our young person what he or she doesn't want to hear, and that's the dreaded two-letter word *no*.

As parents we tell our kids no and God, who is ultimately the best Father, tells us no too from time to time. The question is, why? Why do we tell our kids no? Why does God tell us no? And how many of us have ever looked at our children and said, "Because I said so"? I discovered that these four words work well on young children and not so much on older ones because they want to know why.

In my view, for every "no" or "don't" in the Bible, God always had a better "yes" and "do." I can say, as someone who has ministered to thousands of teenagers, that we must teach our younger generation that God has many more yes than no answers in store for them. In fact, he doesn't thrive on telling his children no. He thrives in directing them to his great yes.

A good example is when we guide teenagers in the world of dating. For a young person who is striving to live godly, there will be people God and a daddy say no to. However, this no isn't intended to deprive our children of a relationship, but it is intended for their protection and ultimately to see them marry God's yes. It is ultimately good to remind our children that rules preserve our relationships both with God and with each other.

Finally, 1 Timothy 6:11 is a verse I often use when ministering to teenagers. "But you, man of God, *flee* from all this, and *pursue* righteousness, godliness, faith, love, endurance and gentleness" (emphasis added). Here in one verse the apostle Paul summed up a perspective concerning the nature of God's commands in Scripture. Simply stated, Christianity isn't just about the absence of evil; it's about the presence of good (and God) in our lives. It is about both fleeing the bad and pursuing the good.

Sometimes as parents and even as ministers, we have unintentionally depicted Christianity as focused only on keeping our lives free from evil. This is only half of the truth. We also must teach people, especially our children, that Christianity is about pursuing what is good and seeking God's best for our lives. This two-fold perspective on the gospel ensures that I will present the positive aspects of following Christ. It will also help me establish common ground with my kids.

Fighting for Common Ground

Establishing common ground with your child or teen is the first part of discipling your own children. Some might disagree and say, "No, taking them to church is" or "Doing a devotional together" is the first aspect of raising godly kids. Certainly these tasks are vital, necessary, and valuable parts of raising godly children. However, parents are the primary spiritual influence on their children—more so than friends and more even than the local church. And so for me, I try to work hard to remain in close relationship with my children because I desire for them to see Christ in me first.

At a recent conference, a father approached me with both frustration and fear in his eyes and said, "I like to hunt, and all my boy likes to do is play Xbox. What do you expect me to do?" With compassion I said, "Find a hunting game and play it with him on his Xbox!" My point was, do whatever it takes to establish common ground with your teenager. You already know kids are different these days, and many of their favorite activities now center on their smartphones and the Internet, making it harder to find things you enjoy doing together. However, common ground is essential to building your relationship with your child. If our kids know us only as the disciplinarian or the busy parent (I too have struggled with being a busy parent), speaking into their lives, especially about tough life lessons, will become increasingly difficult.

The common ground you establish with your children can only help them establish a relationship with Christ. The reason is really nothing profound. It is through the things we enjoy doing the most together that my kids get to see me live out an authentic Christian life.

One area of common ground I have with my boys is sports. They are both big-time baseball players, but together we all enjoy backyard football. I've spent many evenings playing with them in our backyard, which we have named the BABY, the Broken-Ankle Back Yard (you football and basketball players understand the name). When my sons were toddlers, playing in the backyard was all about pure fun. However, you won't believe how competitive these games are now, especially when all the neighborhood boys show up for game day.

I can't tell you how much laughter, not to mention how many life and biblical lessons, I've shared with my boys. For example, trash talk seems to be second nature with boys. But it's also been a great arena to speak to them about the power of our words. I've also noticed that boys tend to bend the rules to benefit themselves in our backyard. This has been a great opportunity to speak into their lives about integrity. Constantly, if a play is close, I will challenge one of my boys to "just be honest and be a man of integrity." Since they know lying is a cardinal sin in our home, it's amazing how many opportunities they've had to exercise good, old-fashioned honesty, even if it costs them a touchdown. And lastly, my boys are watching my attitude, hearing my words, and constantly observing my reactions. There are times when I fail and must take ownership, but for the most part I've made a solid commitment that my boys will see me live Christ within our common ground. I believe modeling Christian behavior in front of them will greatly influence their own faith.

Discipling Your Own Child along Life's Road

When I'm close to my kids, this closeness provides me the opportunity to speak into their lives and connect everyday moments to God's word. And please take note: even at times when we don't necessarily feel as close to our children as we would like, we still have every right to promote God's word because we are their parents.

When I speak at summer youth camps, my encouragement to the counselors is simply, "Play hard with them during the day, and you will be able to pray hard with them about their lives during the services at night." The same concept can be translated into our parenting. By playing with them I don't mean becoming more of a friend to them than a parent. By no means! And by no means am I saying that as a parent you have to "earn" their respect. However, a relationship is the best breeding ground for mutual respect to grow. And when I have their respect, they listen to me when the opportunity presents itself in everyday life.

I'll never forget the time when my sons, Jake and Josh at ages four and five, collected what seemed to be every acorn in our backyard. They were so proud and exclaimed, "Look, Daddy, here are some acorns." I looked at them and said, "No, boys, those are oak trees." They laughed and said, "No, Daddy, acorns!" We went back and forth, but then I was able to say to them that those tiny acorns could be oak trees one day. I was able to talk to them about God as a creator and then compare them to those acorns; they were something small now, but they were able to grow into something mighty over time. I shared with them that there is even a Bible verse in the book of Isaiah that calls us "oaks of righteousness." Their faces lit up, and on some level they got it.

I'm sure some of my enthusiasm about that little lesson went straight over Jake and Josh's heads. However, it was one of those moments as a parent when a light bulb went on. Not only should I do devotions with my kids at night, but life itself is a devotional with plenty of windows each day, through which we can view God and his word. And sure enough, as my boys have gotten older, some of the lessons have become weightier in nature. Whether it's seeing the school bully as a child who needs Jesus or becoming focused and breaking free from some insecurity, I've found that my relationship with them is the currency that gives me a greater platform to speak into their lives. The same is true for your children or future children as well. It's time to become excited again about seizing everyday moments to bring spiritual truths to our kids.

Conclusion

This might seem like a strange way to end a book, but I'm convicted more than ever about the words of Joshua becoming the standard of my home. "As for me and my house, we will serve the Lord." The truth is, a life that wins will win others and influence them toward Christ. The first and most important arena of influence, however, will be my own home. I want to live a winning life, because I want to win my own kids to Christ.

How about You?

Yesterday I challenged you to think about another hinge decision to consider beyond today. Today I would like you to focus on your family for a few minutes. Much of today's reading centers on the relationship you have with your kids. (For those without kids, hopefully this book has challenged you to dream a bit about the kind of relationship you would like to have with your future children.) Take a moment to think about the areas of common ground you share with each child. Ask God to help you connect everyday moments to him or her as opportunities present themselves. For further resources, please visit http://www.reachthecity.com/equip. God bless you as you strive to live a life that wins! May you win others and influence them for Christ!

APPENDIX

WEEK 1
Sermon Outline: Moving on a "Maybe"
1 Samuel 14:1–6

Introduction

Jesus came to give us a full and abundant life right now. John 10:10 says, "The thief comes to steal, kill, and to destroy, but I have come that you might have life and have it to the full." We all have the choice to make biblical decisions that will help us to fully experience the abundant life we are meant to live. Through this campaign, you are challenged to make a hinge decision, which is simply defined as a small decision that will open doors for you. During the campaign we will focus on decisions that will fall into six categories:

- Our F__________________.
- Our F__________________.
- Our F__________________.
- Our F__________________.
- Our F__________________.
- Our F__________________.

One key point to remember—Decide b__________________ by thinking s__________________!

Through this book, a small group series, and a campaign we will be focusing on six principles of a winning life. Today we will be looking at our first principle, decisiveness, which is best illustrated from the life of Jonathan and his young armor-bearer in 1 Samuel 14:1–6. We will discover four character traits for every person who moves on a "maybe" and follows through with his or her hinge decision.

> Now it happened one day that Jonathan the son of Saul said to the young man who bore his armor, "Come, let us go over to the Philistines' garrison that is on the other side." But he did not tell his father. And Saul was sitting in the outskirts of Gibeah under a pomegranate tree which is in Migron. The people who were with him were about six hundred men. Ahijah the son of Ahitub, Ichabod's brother, the son of Phinehas, the son of Eli, the Lord's priest in Shiloh, was wearing an ephod. But the people did not know that Jonathan had gone. Between the passes, by which Jonathan sought to go over to the Philistines' garrison, there was a sharp rock on one side and a sharp rock on the other side. And the name of one was Bozez, and the name of the other Seneh. (1 Sam. 14:1–4 NKJV)

1. People who move on a "maybe" determine that one day must become t_____________.

First Samuel 14:1 says, "Now it happened one day that Jonathan the son of Saul said to the young man who bore his armor, 'Come, let us go over to the Philistines' garrison that is on the other side.' But he did not tell his father" (NKJV).

- Pop quiz: Do you tend to procrastinate? Are you a creature of habit?
- People who fulfill their hinge decisions are people who move on their decisions today, not tomorrow. In fact, the greatest enemy of today is tomorrow.

2. People who move on a "maybe" don't tell their f____________________.

"Don't tell their father" means they don't allow their past to affect their present.

Paul said in Philippians 3:13, "One thing I do, forgetting what is behind, and straining toward what is ahead." Not allowing the past to control you is so important that Paul said it is the "one thing" he made the decision to do in order to make the most of his present.

3. People who move on a "maybe" choose ________ over________.

Throughout this forty-day campaign, you are challenged to journey with one accountability partner who will

- ask you the hard questions;
- bear your burdens as his or her own; and
- pray for you.

4. People who move on a "maybe" come out of the h________ they tend to hide in.

Did you play hide-and-seek as a kid? There are two things that are usually said when one plays this childhood favorite:

- Come out, come out, ______________________________!
- Ready or not, __________________________________!

God the Father doesn't want us hiding in holes such as fear and anxiety. We need to be moving when Christ returns for his church.

Closing Questions

1. What is the one hinge decision you're making during this forty-day campaign, and what small decisions are you making to bring it into reality?
2. Who is the one person in your life who could serve as a young armor-bearer (accountability partner), the one walking with you and holding you accountable throughout Reach the City?
3. What hole do you tend to hide in? What issues, pains, and hurts from your past could keep you from seizing your present and moving forward into your future?

WEEK 1
Small Group Outline: Decisiveness and Personal Outreach

First Samuel 14:6 says, "One day Jonathan son of Saul said to his young armor-bearer, 'Come, let's go over to the Philistine outpost on the other side.'"

Introduction—Comparing Personal Outreach to a Railroad Track

In this series you are being challenged to have two discussions with one unchurched person in your life. Think of personal outreach as a railroad track. Just as there are two rails that comprise a railroad track, there are two discussions that comprise reaching your unchurched friends. We must share Christ in two ways:

- Show Christ with your friend through a Matthew Party.
- Share Christ with your__by inviting them to a Friends and Family Day church service.

Key Decisions When It Comes to Sharing Your Faith

1. The Decision to P________________________________.

Two powerful prayers you can pray for yourself are found in Colossians 4:3–4.

Colossians 4:3 says, "And pray for us, too, that God may open a door for our message, so that we may proclaim the mystery of Christ, for which I am in chains. Pray that I may proclaim it clearly as I should."

Open d______________________________________.
Clear p______________________________________.

2. The Decision to P

Matthew 9:36 tells us how Jesus viewed the lost. "When he saw the crowds, he had compassion on them, because they were harassed and helpless, like sheep without a shepherd."

3. The Decision to P______________________________

Luke 19:10 says, "For the Son of Man came to seek and to save the lost."

Luke 15:4 says, "Does he not leave all the 99 in the open country and *go after the lost sheep, until he finds it*" (emphasis added).

First Samuel 14:6 says, "Come, let's go over to the outpost of those uncircumcised men. Perhaps the Lord will act in our behalf. Nothing can hinder the Lord from saving, whether by many or by few."

First Samuel 14:6 says, "Come, let us go over to the garrison of these uncircumcised; it may be that the Lord will work for us" (NKJV, emphasis added).

4. The Decision to P______________________________.

Second Corinthians 5:20 says, "We are therefore Christ's ambassadors, as though God were making his appeal through us."

Romans 10:14 says, "How, then, can they call on the one they have not believed in? And how can they believe in the one of whom they have not heard. And how can they hear without someone preaching to them. And how can anyone preach, unless they are sent? As it is written, 'How beautiful are the feet of those who bring good news!'"

The gospel is g_____n_____.
The story must be told with the following:
S____
____
S

- He C____________________________________.
- He D____________________________________.
- He R_______________________A_______________
.

And with a S______________________________!

5. The Decision to P ______________________________
____

Luke 15:7 says, "I tell you that in the same way there will be more rejoicing in heaven over one sinner who repents than over ninety-nine righteous persons who don't need to repent."

- M_____Party (Luke 5:27–32)
- S______Party (Luke 15:7,10, 32)
- B______Party (Acts 2:38)

Small Group Discussion Questions

1. For those comfortable with sharing, what is your hinge decision during this forty-day campaign? Who is the one unchurched person in your life you are committing to reach over the next forty days?
2. Which of the five decisions from today's session will be the easiest for you? The hardest? Why?

3. Do you feel like you're decisive on following through on your hinge decision and your commitment to reach one unchurched friend?
4. As a small group, brainstorm the best idea for a corporate Matthew Party.

Small Group Reminders/Small Group Leader Tips

- Remind them of key dates.
  - Three Days of Outreach
  - Small Group Matthew Party
  - Friends and Family Day
  - Serve the City Saturday
- Small Group Will Meet Every Week at

WEEK 2
Sermon Outline: Victory in the Valley
1 Samuel 17:17–58

Introduction

The goal of this series is to help all of us become more intentional in living a Christian life. Remember, a winning life will win others. When we become more intentional, we will also become more influential in the lives of those who don't know Christ.

This week we're going to talk about principle two, personal drive, which the story of David and Goliath in 1 Samuel 17:17–58 best illustrates.

Hebrews 12:1–2 says, "Therefore, since we are surrounded by such a great cloud of witnesses, let us throw off everything that hinders and the sin that so easily entangles, and let us run with perseverance the race marked out for us."

The Amplified Bible defines the word *perseverance* as "patient e_______________or steady and active p________________________."

1. David was driven by a "____________________________."

Author Simon Sinek writes that when it comes to change, we must always start with "Why?" In other words, to fulfill any decision, we must have a deep comprehension of the reasons we need change in the first place. David set out to destroy Goliath because he wanted to restore a sense of self-respect within God's people while ensuring that God's name was also held in honor. This was David's "why," and it ran deep within him.

Our "why" must run deep within our h ____________________ when it comes to change.

2. David was driven by a "______________________."

First Samuel 17:14 says, "David was the youngest. The three oldest followed Saul, but David went back and forth from Saul to tend his father's sheep at Bethlehem." So there David was, the youngest, serving Saul as a future king and then going back to serve his father as a shepherd. David was somewhere in the middle, between his p____and his f___ potential.

3. David was driven by the "________________."

First Samuel 17:14 says, "David was the youngest. The three oldest followed Saul, but David went back and forth from Saul to tend his father's sheep at Bethlehem."

David was somewhere in the middle, between his p ________and his f ______________ potential.

4. Also, be driven by the "________________________."

Hebrews 11:6 says, "He is a rewarder of those who diligently seek Him."

Good goals…

- are s______________ and measurable;
- have a time frame and a d________________;
- are accomplished through p______________ behavior;
- are accomplished through b______________ behaviors;
- are i____________________; and
- are w______________ d________________.

5. And David was driven by the "____________________."

The Bible says that David faced Goliath in a valley. David saw this location as a place for God to do a mighty work. It was a matter of perspective. The same is true for us.

- First, don't focus on how thick the door is. focus on being f___ with just the one small hinge decision you have made.
- Second, don't focus on how giant Goliath is. Focus on how giant your G___is.
- And third, remember that the greater the valley, the greater the v________________________________.

Conclusion

We cannot allow anything to hinder us when it comes to defeating the Goliaths of our lives. We must remain driven, even when we hear the many voices that will mock us along the way. Especially when we seek to fulfill the second aspect of the 1-2-3 Challenge, the challenge is to do the following:

- Share Christ with your life by inviting your critics to a Matthew Party.
- Share Christ with your lips by inviting them to church on Friends and Family Day scheduled for (date)_____.

Closing Questions

1. What drives you the most to fulfill your hinge decision? Is it the "why," the "who," the "where," the "how," or the "where"? Which one drives you the least?

2. Take a minute and dream about what life might look like once your decision is fulfilled. What practical rewards could come your way by fulfilling your hinge decision? Write down at least three rewards.
3. What does the voice of opposition say to you the most when it comes to taking risks for God and setting out to fulfill spiritual commitments? For example, "You have tried this before and failed" and "You aren't really that serious." How can you fight this voice?

WEEK 2
Small Group Outline: Developing Personal Drive for Personal Outreach

This week we're looking at the principle of drive from the story of David and Goliath. There are three things that should drive us to reach the unchurched: ____________________ should drive us.

Luke 16:19–24 says,

> There was a rich man who was dressed in purple and fine linen and lived in luxury every day. At his gate was laid a beggar named Lazarus, covered with sores and longing to eat what fell from the rich man's table. Even the dogs came and licked his sores. The time came when the beggar died and the angels carried him to Abraham's side. The rich man also died and was buried. In Hades, where he was in torment, he looked up and saw Abraham far away, with Lazarus by his side. So he called to him, "Father Abraham, have pity on me and send Lazarus to dip the tip of his finger in water and cool my tongue, because I am in agony in this fire." But Abraham replied, "Son, remember that in your lifetime you received your good things, while Lazarus received bad things, but now he is comforted here and you are in agony."

____should drive us.

Matthew 28:18–20 says, "All authority in heaven and on earth has been given to me. Therefore go and make disciples of all nations, baptizing them in the name of the Father and of the Son and of the Holy Spirit, and teaching them to obey everything I have commanded you. And surely I am with you always, to the very end of the age."

Mark 16:15 says, "Go into all the world and preach the gospel to all creation."

- The Great Commission isn't a suggestion; it is a c__________.
- Our________________________________with Christ should drive us.

Acts 4:20 says, "For we can not help but to speak about what we have seen and heard."

- My witness should flow from my w____________________.

We cannot allow any of the Great Commission myths to hinder our drive to reach the unchurched.

Great Commission Myths

Myth #1: People accept Christ through__________________.

Truth: People accept Christ through the_____of the gospel.

Romans 10:10–14 says, "How, then, can they call on the one they have not believed in? And how can they believe in the one of whom they have not heard? And how can they hear without someone preaching to them?"

Myth #2: If I share my faith and a person doesn't receive Christ, I have____________________.

Truth: Everyone is at a different stage of____when it comes to receiving Christ.

First Corinthians 3:5–7 says, "I planted the seed, Apollos watered it, but God has been making it grow. So neither the one who plants nor the one who waters is anything, but only God, who makes things grow."

Myth #3: Sharing the gospel is too ________________.

Truth: The entire Christian faith is so simple that it can be shared on a ______________________.

Remember to memorize Romans 6:23. "For the wages of sin is death, but the gift of God is eternal life through Christ Jesus our Lord."

Small Group Discussion Questions

1. What tends to drive you the most to reach people? Is it obedience, eternity, or your personal testimony?
2. What myth can seem to hinder you the most from sharing your faith with others?
3. If you were to spend time with your unchurched friend, what would you invite him or her to do? Go out for lunch, share coffee, or go fishing? What will you do to intentionally spend time with your one unchurched friend during these forty days? Remember, hosting a corporate Matthew Party with your small group is good, but regular time with your friend on an ongoing basis is best.
4. From this week's reading of *A Life That Wins*, what tends to drive you the most to fulfill your one hinge decision?

Small Group Reminders/Small Group Leader Tips

- This week start finalizing the details for your small group Matthew Party. Remind small group members to also plan a one-on-one Matthew Party, in which they spend time with their unchurched friend by eating lunch, grabbing coffee, shopping, fishing, and so forth.
- Remember to use the social media website. The small group leader needs to instruct the group on how to log in to the small group's page.
- Remind them of key dates.
    - Three Days of Outreach
    - Small Group Matthew Party
    - Friends and Family Day
    - Serve the City Saturday
    - Small Group Will Meet Every Week at

WEEK 3
Sermon Outline: This Time!

Genesis 29:31–35

Introduction

Today we will be looking into principle three, direction, which is illustrated in the life of Leah.

The truth is, getting to a "this time" kind of decision that sticks and shapes your life forever will come with time and a process. This is what took place in Leah as she gave birth to each son while moving closer and closer to a lasting difference in her life. Amazingly, the meaning behind each of her son's names signified a different level of her growth and can serve as the same for you.

> When the LORD saw that Leah was not loved, he enabled her to conceive, but Rachel remained childless. Leah became pregnant and gave birth to a son. She named him Reuben, for she said, "It is because the LORD has seen my misery. Surely my husband will love me now." She conceived again, and when she gave birth to a son she said, "Because the LORD heard that I am not loved, he gave me this one too." So she named him Simeon. Again she conceived, and when she gave birth to a son she said, "Now at last my husband will become attached to me, because I have borne him three sons." So he was named Levi. She conceived again, and when she gave birth to a son she said, "This time I will praise the LORD." So she named him Judah. Then she stopped having children. (Gen. 29:31–35)

Blind spots have one of two profound impacts on our lives:

First, just like driving a car, we can usually m________________.

Second, unfinished issues can cause us to play it safe because we know the blind spot exists, yet we are u__or not t ________________ how to deal with it.

1. R

- R____________means "behold a s____________."
- The first level of freedom has to do with our p_________.
- Psalm 139:1–2 says, "You have searched me, Lord, and you know me. You know when I sit and when I rise; you perceive my thoughts from afar."

2. S

- S____________means "one who_______."
- David said in Psalm 3:4, "I cried out to the Lord, and he answered me from His Holy mountain."
- We must learn to pray with transparency and authenticity. God can handle our honesty! He hears us when we cry out to him.

3. L

- L____________means "_______."
- We must understand that applying God's word to our lives detaches us from those things that are unhealthy and attaches us to the love and power of the Holy Spirit in our lives.

4. J

- J_____________ means "_______."
- Genesis 29:35 says, "*This time, I will praise the Lord*" (emphasis added).

Conclusion

God wants our breakthroughs to become p_____ in our lives.

Closing Questions

1. In this season of life, what name do you feel like God would have you learn (Reuben, Simeon, Levi, or Judah)? Which is easiest for you? Hardest?
2. Do you really feel like you have come to a "this time" kind of attitude when it comes to fulfilling your hinge decision?
3. What is one hurt, habit, or hang-up you battle? Do you really believe you can row to a level of permanent freedom in this area? Can "this time" become "all the time?"

WEEK 3
Small Group Outline: Directing the Natural into the Spiritual

Genesis 29:35 says, "This time I will praise the Lord." So she named him Judah.

Leah came to the decision that her self-esteem wouldn't be based on how someone else (Jacob) responded to her. We must do the same when it comes to personal outreach. Our self-esteem and how we view ourselves aren't based on our "performance" or on how well we share our faith. Our confidence is based solely on who we are in Christ and on who he is in us. In fact, our willingness and obedience to share Christ define success with personal outreach, not how someone responds to us. We must have a "this time" attitude when it comes to outreach. The right perspective will relieve us of our insecurity and the undue pressure we may feel.

Spiritual dialogue can follow the following format:

- I________________________________to church
- Make sure you c____________the invitation. Remember, your excitement about your church is contagious.

C___________________________about religion/spirituality

After the invitation, learn to ask "leading questions." A leading question or statement is simply the next thing you say after your friend responds to your invitation. For example:

- Did you grow up in church?
- Do you consider yourself to be a very religious person?
- Has anybody ever told you the difference between Christianity and "religion"?

P______________________________of the gospel

- The gospel on a napkin
- Whether you use the gospel on a napkin or any other format for sharing your faith, the goal is a clear presentation that communicates the full gospel message. The full message can easily be remembered with three Ss—Sin, Savior, and Surrender.
- All have sinned and fallen short of what it takes to get into heaven. Not only that, but God in his justice has punished sin with spiritual death.
- The reason Christ came was to pay the penalty of our sin (death) by dying on the cross for us. God so hates sin that he punishes it with death, but he so loves us that he sent us his Son as our Savior.
- We must accept Christ as our Savior and surrender our lives to him as our Lord.

The Gospel on a Napkin

The goal of the gospel on a napkin is to offer you a simple and easy-to-remember strategy for sharing your faith. It is based on one verse in the Bible, Romans 6:23, and it provides a visual illustration of the entire Christian faith…on a napkin. Even if you never actually use a napkin, you can memorize the verse and the content for each of the six key words below as an easy way to remember the central truths of the gospel message. I encourage you to practice this method until you can fluently share the gospel with a friend.

Step 1: Write out the verse at the top of the napkin and draw out the two ledges.

Romans 6:23 says, "For the wages of sin is death, but the gift of God is eternal life through Christ Jesus our Lord."

Step 2: Circle the word *wages* and write it at the top of the left-hand ledge.

Explain that wages are simply what we earn for something we've done. Everyone who has a job understands wages. Your pay is what you've earned for what you've done.

Step 3: Circle the word *sin* and write it beneath the word wages.

Explain that the wages of sin (what we've earned for what we've done) is death. Then give a definition of sin. Sin is doing the things God has declared as wrong. Sin is disobedience to God's ways and choosing our way over his.

Step 4: Circle the word *death* and write it beneath the word *sin.*

Explain that this isn't just a physical death (resulting from the fall of mankind) but a spiritual death that has separated us from the presence of God in our lives. God created us to be in close relationship with him, but because of sin, we are now separated from his presence, and the penalty of sin is upon our lives. If we remain separated from him when we die, we will go to a place called hell—which is ultimately eternal separation from God.

Step 5: Circle the word *but* and write it between the two ledges at the bottom of the chasm.

Point out the word *but.* At least for our illustration, it suggests there is good news.

Step 6: Draw a stick figure on top of the left-hand ledge.

This little guy represents a life separated from God. You can refer back to him from this point forward as you explain how someone separated from God is able to cross over from spiritual death to spiritual life.

Step 7: Circle the word *gift* and write it at the top of the ledge on the right-hand side of the napkin.

At this point start drawing a comparison between the words on the left with the words on the right. Explain that while *wages* is on the left-hand ledge, the word *gift* is directly opposite it on the right-hand side. Draw a difference between *wages* and *gift.* Wages are what you get for something you've done, but a gift is something you receive based on what someone else paid for. Wages are earned, but gifts are free to you because someone else paid for them.

Step 8: Circle the words *of God* and write them under the word gift.

Draw a comparison to the word *sin* on the left side and *of God* on the right. On one side there is sinfulness, but on the other side is a sinless God who has an amazing gift for mankind. Highlight the reality that this gift is "of God," a holy and righteous yet loving God who desires for us all to become his children. Go as far as saying, "If you and I love to receive something we've been desiring from someone on earth, how much more should we desire a gift that is 'of God'?"

Step 9: Circle eternal *life* and write it under *of God.*

Again, draw a final contrast between the word *death* on the left side and *eternal life* on the right side. Although we deserve death ("the wages of sin is death"), this gift of God is eternal life. His gift to us is the opportunity to spend eternity in heaven.

Step 10: Draw a cross bridging the gap between the two ledges and circle the phrase "Christ Jesus our Lord."

Write in "Christ Jesus our Lord" somewhere in the cross. Draw an arrow showing the stick figure crossing over from the ledge on the left to the ledge on the right. Communicate that we cross over by giving the lordship of our life to Christ. Explain that three days after his crucifixion, God raised Christ back to life.[1]

Closing

Once finishing the illustration, ask whether your friend has any questions. After engaging in any other necessary conversation, ask him or her, "Is there any reason why you wouldn't want to cross over from spiritual death to spiritual life and become a Christian today?" Allow him or her to answer. If your friend communicates that he or she is ready to make the decision, lead him or her in a very simple prayer, in which your friend asks Jesus to forgive him or her of his or her sin and become the Lord of his or her life.

If not, tell him or her that you understand it's a big decision. Request to meet with your friend again in a week so you can answer any questions he or she may have. If he or she does accept Christ, immediately offer to meet with him or her weekly to help guide your friend in his or her spiritual growth. Compel your friend to visit your church, communicate the importance of water baptism, and offer him or her a free Bible. Do everything you can to help assimilate your friend into the family of God and help him or her grow spiritually.

Small Group Discussion Questions

1. How likely do you believe your friend is going to attend your church at least once?
2. What are the positive aspects about your church that you feel people need to hear? Remember, "contextualize" the invitation. Point out the aspects of your church that you believe your unchurched friend(s) would really enjoy.
3. How easy does it seem to share the gospel on a napkin? What are parts of the illustration that might seem like a "stretch" for you to share?
4. As a small group, divide into pairs and practice sharing the gospel on a napkin.

Small Group Reminders/Small Group Leader Tips

- Finalize and announce the date for your small group Matthew Party.
- Remind your group about your Friends and Family Day service, which is happening very soon.
- Remember to use the social media website. The small group leader needs to instruct the group on how to log in to the small group's page.

- Remind them of key dates.
- Three Days of Outreach
- Small Group Matthew Party
- Friends and Family Day
- Serve the City Saturday
- Small Group Will Meet Every Week at

WEEK 4
Sermon Outline: A Pivotal Place

Genesis 28:10–22

Principle four, dependency, comes from the life of the Old Testament character Jacob. Genesis 28:10–22 says,

> Jacob left Beersheba and set out for Harran. When he reached a certain place, he stopped for the night because the sun had set. Taking one of the stones there, he put it under his head and lay down to sleep. He had a dream in which he saw a stairway resting on the earth, with its top reaching to heaven, and the angels of God were ascending and descending on it. There above it stood the Lord, and he said: "I am the Lord, the God of your father Abraham and the God of Isaac. I will give you and your descendants the land on which you are lying. Your descendants will be like the dust of the earth, and you will spread out to the west and to the east, to the north and to the south. All peoples on earth will be blessed through you and your offspring. I am with you and will watch over you wherever you go, and I will bring you back to this land. I will not leave you until I have done what I have promised you." When Jacob awoke from his sleep, he thought, "Surely the Lord is in this place, and I was not aware of it." He was afraid and said, "How awesome is this place! This is none other than the house of God; this is the gate of heaven." Early the next morning Jacob took the stone he had placed under his head and set it up as a pillar and poured oil on top of it. He called that place Bethel, though the city used to be called Luz. Then Jacob made a vow, saying, "If God will be with me and will watch over me on this journey I am taking and will give me food to eat and clothes to wear so that I return

> safely to my father's household, then the Lord will be my God and this stone that I have set up as a pillar will be God's house, and of all that you give me I will give you a tenth."

The word *pivotal* means "key, essential, critical, and important." When you find yourself at any kind of pivotal place in life, the question you must answer is, "Which way do I lean?"

Proverbs 3:5–6 says, "Trust in the Lord with all your heart, and *lean* not on your own understanding. In all your ways acknowledge Him and he will make your paths straight" (emphasis added). Which way are you leaning in life? On your own understanding? On your own ability to self-govern your life and circumstances? Or do you depend on God?

1. God teaches dependence by giving a d______________.

- God doesn't give p___________people dreams; he gives I _____________people dreams so they will learn to depend on him.
- God speaks to us out of "our completed state." He speaks to us not *as we are* but a ____________. He will give a glimpse of our "future self" to help us endure the transformation process.

2. God teaches dependence on him by allowing us to face his d __________.

- Hebrews 12:7 says, "Endure hardship as discipline; God is treating you as his children." God tells us to treat hardship as_____.
- We must understand that God defines "good discipline" as "g ____."
- Jesus himself defined spiritual success as the one who is the least and s _________ the most. Matthew 25:40 and Philippians 2:7

3. God teaches dependence through____that causes us to limp.

- God asked Jacob a pointed question in Genesis 32:27. "What is your _________?"
- If there is one takeaway truth from today's message, it is this: we will never become what we can be until we admit who we really______________________________________.

Conclusion

It would have been great if Jacob's journey had been a bed of roses from this point forward. But the truth is, Jacob had to continue growing into his new name. So do you and I. It is definitely great to make tremendous strides, but dependence is a daily decision and something we learn again and again with each season of life we face.

Closing Questions

1. Have you ever thought about the truth that God will teach us to depend on him through the dreams he has for our lives?
2. What difficulties are you currently facing that God will use to teach you a greater level of dependence?
3. Do you agree that God will sometimes allow his children to limp through certain seasons of life? Why or why not? Do you find yourself in a season of limping?

WEEK 4
Small Group Outline: Dependence on God for Personal Outreach

Welcome to Week 4 of our personal outreach series. This week we will explore dependence as it relates to personal outreach. The truth is, we cannot reach people on our own. We need the help of the Holy Spirit and his power to make our efforts to reach others powerful and effective. This week we will look at Peter, the very first person with the honor of publicly preaching about Jesus Christ after the church was born on the day of Pentecost in the book of Acts. I think we can learn a lot from the guy who, in the previous season of his life, denied Jesus to a junior high girl at a campfire and in the very next season preached to three thousand people, who got saved. Peter learned to depend on the Holy Spirit, and as a result, the denier was turned into a declarer.

Acts 2: 14 says, "Then Peter stood up with the Eleven, raised his voice and addressed the crowd." He then proceeded to present the gospel, and his presentation resulted in the following response in Acts 2:37: "When the people heard this, they were cut to the heart and said to Peter and the other apostles, 'Brothers, what shall we do?'" Through depending on the Holy Spirit, his outreach to others had a profound impact. Our outreach can have an impact too. In this lesson we will glean some practical insight from Peter's presentation in the book of Acts.

1. Understand that God's___is with you as you share your faith.

Genesis 1:2–3 says, "Now the earth was formless and empty, darkness was over the surface of the deep, and the Spirit of God was hovering over the waters. And God said, 'Let there be light,' and there was light."

2. Trust God to o__________________________doors for you.

3. We have to use s_____strategically when we share our faith.

Romans 6:23 says, "For the wages of sin is death, but the gift of God is eternal life in Christ Jesus our Lord."

Romans 3:23 says, "For all have sinned and fall short of the glory of God."

Romans 5:8 says, "But God demonstrates his own love for us in this: While we were still sinners, Christ died for us."

4. Explain the b_______________________________words.

Examples:

Small Group Discussion Questions

1. How easy is it for you to depend on God when it comes to personal outreach? Do you really believe that God will help you share the gospel as you try to share your faith?
2. How can you tell when doors are open for you to share your faith? How can you tell when they are wide open, slightly cracked, or slammed shut?
3. If you could communicate some of your favorite life verses with your unchurched friend, what would they be?

Small Group Reminders/Small Group Leader Tips

- This is a big week! Friends and Family Day is next Sunday. Spend time praying for this special day and reminding your small group members to invite their unchurched friends to church.
- Your Serve the City Saturday is likely happening next week as well. Make sure small group members are clear as to where they are volunteering to serve during this special day.
- Remember to use the social media website. The small group leader needs to instruct the group on how to log in to the small group's page.
- Remind them of key dates.
  - Three Days of Outreach
  - Small Group Matthew Party
  - Friends and Family Day
  - Serve the City Saturday
  - Small Group Will Meet Every Week at

WEEK 5
Sermon Outline: Here Comes That Dreamer!
Genesis 37:19–20

Introduction

Principle five is dreaming. Perhaps no other Bible story better illustrates the way God develops our dreams over time than the life of Joseph.

Living out our dreams can be a difficult journey. Through the life of Joseph, we can learn three critical choices we can make in the midst of a difficulty journey toward dream fulfillment.

Genesis 37:19–20 says, "'Here comes that dreamer!' they said to each other. 'Come now, let's kill him and throw him into one of these cisterns and say that a ferocious animal devoured him. Then we'll see what comes of his dreams.'"

1. Though he was d ____________, he never d________ God.

Every dream goes through seasons of "denial" or opposition.

- The response of o__________________ to our dream can serve as one form of opposition.
- Dreams take r ______________ and h________________ work.

Eleanor Roosevelt said, "Do one thing every day that scares you!"

2. He chose c_____________at all costs.

- Day after day, Joseph lived out the old adage: Sow a t _______, reap an a _____________; sow an a___________________________, reap a h ______________; sow a h______, reap a c____; sow a c__________________________________, reap a d_________.
- Keep reminding yourself that when you feel_____by man, God does not reject you.

3. He understood his dream had to become more about o______________ and less about h________________.

Genesis 50:20 says, "He says to his brothers, reassuring them again, 'You intended to harm me, but God intended it for good to accomplish what is now being done, the saving of many lives.'"

- In one statement Joseph declared that God was at work behind the s_________________ when he couldn't s________________ it.
- In one statement Joseph stated a mature t_______________i n the Lord (Rom. 8:28).
- In this one statement Joseph again released his brothers from their guilt and extended f ____________________to them.
- And finally, this one statement by Joseph acknowledged that the purpose of his long-ago dream was to s_______________ many lives. In this way Joseph pointed to the biggest dream of all in the Bible, which is God's dream to save lives.

Conclusion

Take the opportunity to do two things this morning. First, rededicate your dreams to God. Second, dedicate your life to God.

Closing Questions

1. What is your dream in this season of life?
2. What has been the biggest form of opposition you've faced?
3. What kind of character traits does your dream demand you have?
4. How can your dream result in others being reached?

Week 5
Small Group Outline: The Willingness to Dream

This week we are looking at dream development from the life of Joseph. He is known as one of the greatest dreamers in the entire Bible, yet his dream was ultimately about saving others. At the conclusion of a long and weary process of dream development, Joseph said in Genesis 50:20, "You intended to harm me, but God intended it for good to accomplish what is now being accomplished, the saving of many lives." Let's look into the nature of dreaming from a biblical standpoint and how our dreams, in their final fulfillment, should ultimately reach others as a primary objective.

1. Inspiration for your dream might come from h____________ places but is developed in the d ________________places.

- It is not what you do w________________that will get you into the deep places; it is what you are doing r________________.
- Deep places bring forth__________*b*rings forth but desperation.

2. Dreamers become i______________________________ as they wait upon the Lord.

Isaiah 40:31 says, "But those who wait on the Lord shall renew their strength; They shall mount up with wings like eagles, they shall run and not be weary, they shall walk and not faint" (NKJV).

Remember the six areas of hinge decisions:

- F
- F
- F

- F
- F
- F________________________________

3. Over time dreamers realize the dream is less about them and more about others.

Part of our dream should be developing biblical values within our own family or children. Here are some values I (Mike Holt) try to instill in my children:

- "Nothing is impossible with God."
- "Always encourage others."
- "Forgive freely."

4. Dreamers prioritize their f________________________ as part of their dream.

Small Group Discussion Questions

1. Take a moment to share one of your dreams with your small group.
2. Describe some potential "deep places" you might have to endure on your way to fulfill your dream.
3. What are some specific values you desire to develop in your children?
4. How can God use your dream to reach those who don't know him?

Small Group Reminders/Small Group Leaders Tips

- Rejoice together for the success of your Friends and Family Day and Serve the City Saturday. Reflect on these two days together.
- This week serves as the first week of follow-up for all guests who visited the church last week and individuals ministered to during Serve the City. Encourage your small group members to intentionally follow up with their friends by spending time with them and offering to answer any questions they may have about the church and following Christ.
- Next week would be a great week to invite guests to participate in your small group. We will be talking about the disciplines of the Christian faith, and this is a great week for seekers or new believers to attend.

Week 6
Sermon Outline: Dos and Don'ts of Discipline

Joshua 6:1–6

Introduction

We find principle six, discipline, in the life of Joshua and the battle of Jericho.

Discipline can be looked at as both "don't" and "do." Many people have a negative taste in their mouths when it comes to discipline because all they see are the "don'ts" of the Bible. The truth is, for every no in the Bible, there is a greater yes. And for every don't, there is a do. Joshua 6:1–6 says,

> Now the gates of Jericho were securely barred because of the Israelites. No one went out and no one came in. Then the Lord said to Joshua, "See, I have delivered Jericho into your hands, along with its king and its fighting men. March around the city once with all the armed men. Do this for six days. Have seven priests carry trumpets of rams' horns in front of the ark. On the seventh day, march around the city seven times, with the priests blowing the trumpets. When you hear them sound a long blast on the trumpets, have the whole army give a loud shout; then the wall of the city will collapse and the army will go up, everyone straight in." So Joshua son of Nun called the priests and said to them, "Take up the ark of the covenant of the Lord and have seven priests carry trumpets in front of it."

1. Don't s__________. Do s______________.

- The one sin they battled with the most was m_____________ and c____, which led to unbelief and eventually idolatry.
- Exodus 33:7–11 reveals Joshua's lifelong habit of s _________ t____________in the presence of God.

2. Don't s________________. Do w ____________.

- Two and a half tribes chose the land we could easily call "___."
- To mature as believers:
- W _________________ b _________________
- C________________________a__________________
- M______________________________r___________
- Reading the B _____________________ and praying
- Sharing Christ with others

3. Don't s__________. Do influence your w_______.

- Joshua 24:15 says, "As for me and my house, we will serve the Lord."
- Reaching others begins with our own family and should extend to our friends, extended family, and coworkers.

Conclusion

We will not sin, we will not settle, and we will not stop. We will worship, walk, and influence our world—continuing with our own families.

Closing Questions

1. What is one sin you must make sure doesn't hinder your personal worship from this point forward?
2. Have you ever been tempted to settle in the land of "good enough" instead of continuing to walk after God's very best? What are some reasons believers tend to settle?
3. How will you continue to influence your family and your world for Christ? Who is the next person you will try to reach as we close out the Reach the City campaign?

Week 6
Small Group Outline: The Disciplines of the Christian Faith

Joshua 6:3–4 says, "March around the city once with all the armed men. Do this for six days. Have seven priests carry trumpets of rams' horns in front of the ark. On the seventh day, march around the city seven times, with the priests blowing the trumpets."

In this session we are going to explore the basics of discipling and spiritually mentoring others. Reaching someone for Christ is only the first step. We must help them become mature believers in Christ. And just as you have learned through this campaign that you can reach someone else, you can also mentor (disciple) them. One of the greatest joys you will ever have as a believer this side of heaven is seeing someone grow in his or her faith as a result of your friendship and support.

- The goal is for him or her to become a disciple, which is simply defined as a__________follower of Jesus.
- For anyone to become a disciple, we must answer the question, "______________________________________?" after they give their hearts to Christ.

1. Teach them the importance of_________________________.

Matthew 28:18–20 says, "Then Jesus came to them and said, 'All authority in heaven and on earth has been given to me. Therefore go and make disciples of all nations, baptizing them in the name of the Father and of the Son and of the Holy Spirit, and teaching them to obey everything I have commanded you. And surely I am with you always, to the very end of the age.'"

2. Teach the importance of continuing to ask questions concerning their Christian faith.

- How do I know the Bible is true?

3. Teach the importance of ____________________________ and p _____________________________________.

- Don't forget SOAP.

S
O
A
P

- And remember to PRAY.

P
R
A
Y

4. Teach the importance of biblical c___________________________.

- Hebrews 10:25 says, "Not giving up meeting together, as some are in the habit of doing, but encouraging one another—and all the more as you see the Day approaching."
- Proverbs 27:17 says, "As iron sharpens iron, so one person sharpens another."

5. Teach the discipline of r_______________________ others.

- Teach them the importance of sharing their personal _______
- Your life_________________________________Christ.
- What_____________________has Christ made in your life?
- There is also the "One Thing" testimony. John 9: 25 says, "He replied, 'Whether he is a sinner or not, I don't know. *One thing* I do know. I was blind but now I see!'" (emphasis added).

Small Group Discussion Questions

1. As a small group, turn to Matthew 28:18–20 and have someone read it aloud. Do you agree that everyone in your small group is responsible for fulfilling the Great Commission from this point forward? Part of that Great Commission is making disciples. Do you get excited, nervous, or scared when it comes to carrying the responsibility of spiritually mentoring others?
2. For the next forty days:

    - Where will you read in your Bible from this point forward? What Bible study method or strategy will you follow?
    - How will you continue to reach your one unchurched friend? Who is one more person you can commit to reach from this point forward?

3. Are you comfortable sharing your testimony with others? What format would best suit your testimony? As a small group, have one person share his or her testimony in the three-part format and another person share it in the "one thing" format.

Small Group Reminders/Small Group Leader Tips

Conclude your small group time with each person sharing the one major way this campaign has impacted him or her the most. Brainstorm together your plans to continue meeting, hosting Matthew Parties, and possibly planning another outreach (large or small) in the community *as a small group.*

ENDNOTES

Introduction

[1] Gerry Keller and Jay Papasan, *The ONE Thing: The Surprisingly Simple Truth behind Extraordinary Results* (Austin, TX: Bard Press, 2013), 3.
[2] John Mason, *An Enemy Called Average* (Colorado: David C. Cook, 2003), 3.

Week 1, Day 1

[1] Doctor's Office, Becquet.ca: http://www.becquet.ca/laughter/75.htm

Week 1, Day 3

[1] Stan Martin, "Loving Your Enemies, Don't Tell Daddy page 15, (2003): sermoncentral.com/sermons/ loving-your-enemy-stan-martin
[2] John C. Maxwell, *The 21 Irrefutable Laws of Leadership: Follow Them and People Will Follow You* (Nashville: Thomas Nelson, 2007),

Week 2, Day 1

[1] John Honeycutt, *Daily in the Word* (Striving Together Publications, CA, 2008), 31.
[2] Frank Miniter, *The Ultimate Man's Survival Guide* (Washington DC: Regnery, 2013), 32.

Week 2, Day 2

[1] C. S. Lewis, *The Lion, the Witch, and the Wardrobe* (Grand Rapids, Michigan:HarperCollins, 2002).

[2] Robert Leroe, "The Fear of God," page 1, (1997): sermoncentral.com/sermons/the-fear-of-god-robert-leroe
[3] Os Hillman, "D.L. Moody: A Shoe Salesman", In the Workplace (2006). http://www.intheworkplace.com/apps/articles/default.asp?articleid=12963&columnid=1935.

Week 2, Day 5

[1] Wayne. Cordeiro, The Divine Mentor: Growing Your Faith as You Sit at the Feet of the Savior (Minnesota, Bethany House Publishers, 2008), 101.
[2] Frank R. Shivers, *Christian Basics 101* (Florida, Xulonpress, 2009). 42
[3] K.EdwardSkidmore, "The New and Living Way", page 3, (2005) sermoncentral.com/sermons/the-new-and-living-way-k-edward-ed-skidmore

Week 3, Day 1

[1] Mark Butler, 12th IAAF World Championships in Athletics: IAAF Statistics Handbook (Monaco, International Amateur Athletic Federation, 2009).
[2] Robert Edgerly, Savannah Hauntings; http://www.colorfulplaces.com/destinations/history-of-savannah/
[3] Donald Stamps, General Editor, *The Full Life Study Bible* (Grand Rapids: Zondervan, 1992). 53

Week 3, Day 2

[1] Bob George, *Classic Christianity* (Oregon, Harvest House Publishers, 2010). 107
[2] Thom S. Rainer, *The Unchurched Next Door: Understanding Faith Stages as Keys to Sharing Your Faith* (Grand Rapids: Zondervan, 2009).

Week 3, Day 3

[1] Kelly White, "It's in the Cry," page 2, (2010): sermoncentral.com/sermons/its-in-the- cry-kelly-white
[2] Toby Powers, "Pour It Out," page 2, (2006): sermoncentral.com/sermons/pour-it-out-toby- power-sermons

Week 3, Day 4

[1] Greg Laurie, "An Appointment with a Stranger," Harvest Ministries, September 10, 2013, http://www.harvest.org/devotional/archive/devotion/2013-09-10.

Week 4 Day 1

[1] Donald Stamps, General Editor, *The Full Life Study Bible* (Grand Rapids: Zondervan, 1992). 44

Week 4, Day 2

[1] Brother Lawrence, *Practicing the Presence of God* (Springdale: Merchant Books, 2009).

Week 4, Day 3

[2] Recruit Training: http://www.marines.com/becoming-a-marine/recruit-training/-/twelve-weeks/week/11

Week 4, Day 4

[1] Henry Cloud, *Boundaries: When to Say Yes, How to Say No* (Grand Rapids: Zondervan, 2008), 91.
[2] author unknown, Limitations: short illustrations, Pulpit Helps, 2013.
[3] A. W. Tozer, *The Root of the Righteous* (Chicago, IL, Moody Publishers, 2007), 93.
[4] Charles H. Spurgeon, "Quotable Quote," (2014), https://www.goodreads.com/quotes/764771-great-hearts-can-only-be-made-by-great-troubles-the

Week 4, Day 5

[1] Donald Stamps, General Editor, *The Full Life Study Bible* (Grand Rapids: Zondervan, 1992). 62

Week 5, Day 1

[1] Bill Hybels, *Who You Are When No One's Looking: Choosing Consistency, Resisting Compromise* (Westmont, IL, InterVarsity Press, 1987). 35
[2] Andy Stanley, *Visioneering: God's Blueprint for Developing and Maintaining Vision* (Colorado, WaterBrook Multnomah Publishing, 1999). 18
[3] D. D. Turner, *MSC Health Action News*, July 1993.
[4] 33 Charles Kingsley, "Charles Kingsley quotes," Thinkexist.com, accessed July 4, 2014, http://en.thinkexist.com/quotation/we_act_as_though_comfort_and_luxury_were_the/182212.html.
[5] 34 Jonathan Aitken, *Charles Colson: A Life Redeemed* (Colorado, WaterBrook Multnomah Publising, 2010).

Week 5, Day 3

[1] Michael Jordan, "Failure," retrieved from thoughts.forbes.com.
[2] V. Yap, "Forgiveness: What You Won't Be Sorry For," page 4 (2003): sermoncentral. com/sermons/forgiveness-what-you-wont-be-sorry-for-victor-yap
[3] Bill Petro, "History of Thanksgiving: Friendly Indian?" accessed July 4, 2014, http://billpetro.com/HolidayHistory/hol/squanto.html.

Week 5 Day 4

[1] *The Pursuit of Happiness*, directed by Gabrielle Muccino (2006; Burbank, CA: Columbia Pictures,), DVD.
[2] William Manchester and Paul Reid, *The Last Lion: Winston Spencer Churchill; Defender of the Realm, 1940–1965* (Little, Brown and Company, 2012).
[3] Honor Crowther Fagan, *The Man in the Red Bandanna* http://news.yahoo.com/president-obama-recalls-heroism-man-red-bandana-9-160757580--abc-news-politics.html
[4] Donald Stamps, General Editor, *The Full Life Study Bible* (Grand Rapids: Zondervan, 1992). 71

Week 5, Day 5

[1] Simon Sinek, *Start with Why: How Great Leaders Inspire Everyone to Take Action* (New York, Penguin, 2009).
[2] Les Brown, "Les Brown Quotes," BrainyQuote, accessed July 4, 2014, http://www.brainyquote.com/quotes/authors/l/les_brown.html.
[3] Malcolm Gladwell, *The Tipping Point: How Little Things Can Make a Big Difference* (Little, Brown and Company, 2006).

[4] H. L. Hunt, "H. L. Hunt Quotes," BraindyQuote, accessed July 4, 2014, http://www.brainyquote.com/quotes/authors/h/h_l_hunt.html.
[5] But They Did Not Give Up: http://www.uky.edu/~eushe2/Pajares/OnFailingG.html

Week 6, Day 1

[1] Charles Swindoll, *Living above the Level of Mediocrity* (Nashville: Thomas Nelson, 1989). 124-125

Week 6, Day 4

[1] Dave Ramsey, "Get Ahead of the New Year, Set Goals Now," November 18, 2013, EntreLeadership Podcast.com. http://tunein.com/radio/The-EntreLeadership-Podcast-p344569/

Small Group Outline Week 3

[1] Randy D. Raysbrook, "One-Verse Evangelism," The Navigators Philippines,(2014),http://www.philnavs.org/site/literature/illustrations/oneverseevangelism/.